Discovering Inner Peace

A psychological, philosophical and spiritual perspective

CHRISTINA SAMYCIA, PSYD

authorHOUSE®

AuthorHouse™
1663 Liberty Drive
Bloomington, IN 47403
www.authorhouse.com
Phone: 1-800-839-8640

First published by AuthorHouse 8/31/2009

ISBN: 978-1-4490-1705-7 (e)
ISBN: 978-1-4490-1659-3 (sc)

Printed in the United States of America
Bloomington, Indiana

This book is printed on acid-free paper.

For those who have traveled with me

INTRODUCTION

We are trying to satisfy our external needs, but that is what we don't want. We want an internal Knowledge; we want something that is within, inside of us; we want that inner peace. This is a natural instinct. We are born with that instinct within us, that we are all looking for something in this world. We are all looking, desperately looking.

-Maharaji

Imagine feeling free—free from all those things that create your suffering: your thoughts, your feelings, external stressors, and so many other things. Imagine living a life where you are in control: creating the life that you want, not bound by fear, sadness, or guilt. Imagine feeling strong and powerful; that no matter what may come your way, you can conquer it. Imagine trusting that the universe will lead you where you need to go. Imagine believing that you already have everything you ever needed. This is inner peace.

I can remember the first time I had a glimpse of inner peace. It was a few days after my 35th birthday. I had just returned home from a short get-away to the Bahamas, a present that I had given myself. I was running along the lakefront, as I do just about every morning. For several weeks, I had been contemplating the circumstances of my life. This day, in the middle of my run, as I was assessing all the things that were wrong in my life, something inside of me told me to stop and pause. I looked out at the water. I really looked. At that moment, I found myself totally submerged in the beauty of the scenery. The water was such a deep shade of blue and the sky was so crisp and azure. As I lost myself in the beautiful scene, this feeling came over me—a feeling I had not quite felt before. I was happy; really happy. Not an ecstatic kind of happy, but a peaceful kind of happy. Then I thought to myself, how can I be happy if nothing really happened to me? Nothing in my life had really changed. My life was still the same. I was broke, single, struggling to finish my dissertation so that I could finally graduate, still working hard at losing that ten extra pounds, but despite all that, for just that moment, I found happiness: authentic happiness.

But it was better than happiness. I had found inner peace. For that one beautiful point in time, I was truly in the moment and the moment was perfect because I had accepted the moment for what it truly was. In that moment, I was not thinking of all the things that were wrong because, in essence, at that moment, those things did not exist. The only things that existed at that beautiful moment were me and the world, connected in some way. There was no judgment. I felt that although everything is not where I would like it to be, it is what it was and I could accept it. I finally accepted my life exactly the way that it was and dropped the pain that stemmed from judging and caring about how things weren't at that point. I felt that the place that I belonged was right here and right now. I trusted that everything was going to be okay and that this place that I was in right at that very moment was part of my journey. I felt that all that I had been learning about myself through these experiences culminated in this moment. I finally got it. Right then and there, in the middle of the bike path along Lake Shore Drive, I finally got it.

It was not the pursuit of happiness that I needed, which I had deluded myself to believe. I needed to feel peaceful. I needed to calm all those feelings inside of me that were driving me crazy. I needed to trust that I would be fine even in the midst of the mess that was my life. I found that things that I had always known were missing within me. That emptiness that ate away at me day after day was finally filled. All I had to do was decide to let go of it; let go of what I thought my life should be, let go of trying to change things and let go of the pain. It was so simple, but yet so profound. Why didn't I see this before?

All this time, I believed that I had to try to control and change everything else around me, but now I knew that I really have no control over anything else but me, and that is okay. Is this what they mean about letting go? I realized that inner peace is something that I had been searching for my whole life and I never quite knew it until one chilly Chicago morning. This feeling was something that I had read about before, but had not fully understood what it meant or how profound an experience it was. It was something I knew about, but never truly experienced. Yet when I found it, it was something that I knew I never wanted to release. Now don't get me wrong, there was a long journey that transpired before this epiphany, but this, this was the pivotal moment. It was at that moment that everything came to together and I realized just how simple inner peace can be, when we are ready to let go of ourselves.

We All Search for Inner Peace, Because Each of Us Suffers

Man or woman, young or old, rich or poor: we all suffer. Many philosophers and psychologists assert that life is not merely the pursuit of happiness, but the discovery of inner peace. And we search for inner peace precisely because each of us suffers. We crave it, consciously or otherwise. Each of us experiences feelings of sadness, hurt, anger, anxiety, and disappointment; we feel frustration, loneliness, restlessness, resentfulness, emptiness, and even despair. External stresses, ranging from financial woes to relationship difficulties, negatively affect us all. And these sources of negative emotions create feelings of stress within us. This compels us to search for inner peace, but also blocks us from finding it.

What does inner peace represent? To experience inner peace is to be mentally, physically, and spiritually in a state of harmony, calm, and bliss. It is the feeling of serenity in the face of adversity. Inner peace is an evolved state of being. It is not an emotional state such as happiness, but rather a state of inner knowing, which stabilizes you in times of sorrow, and grounds you in times of elation. As you come to discover inner peace, you will feel empowered. This process will assist you in living more consciously as you learn how to break free from those things that are keeping you from being in control of your life. When you achieve this personal enlightenment, inner peace will follow.

Inner peace is a transformative experience, one that requires a process of personal growth to achieve. You may already have experienced a moment of inner peace. Time seemed to stand still, and you were truly present within that moment. It might have been while witnessing beauty in nature that left you breathless. But most of us have only experienced such peace for a moment because we have not learned how to sustain this inner peace. Wouldn't it be wonderful to experience this inner peace daily? It is precisely the point of this book that this state is in fact possible to achieve. Moreover, the steps outlined below are intended to help you navigate this process.

Finding Inner Peace

The idea of discovering inner peace is not new. It is the fundamental goal of many religions and philosophies, including Buddhism and Taoism. Such approaches emphasize the importance of finding inner peace through a process of self-discovery and transformation. Furthermore, inner peace is important because it provides you control over yourself and, consequently, your life. Through inner peace, we can begin to live consciously and with intention; without it, we are often overwhelmed by thoughts and feelings, some unconscious, others stemming from external sources. As a psychotherapist, I have found that individuals come to therapy because, in some way, they are not feeling at peace. One of the goals of therapy is to assist individuals in discovering this elusive inner peace.

Throughout the course of my personal and professional experiences, I have given much thought to the idea of inner peace. Moreover, I have worked to develop a model of how we can discover it. This process integrates psychological healing, the application of philosophical principles, and an embracing of spirituality. Although the messages in this book are not new, I believe that the methodical integration of these principles leads us to a new way of finding inner peace.

I started to conceptualize this model of inner peace discovery after I noticed that crucial information seemed to be lacking within philosophical and spiritual teachings. Although in most such teachings the psychological principles are implied, they lack detailed information about how to actually heal psychologically. I contend that psychological, philosophical, and spiritual components need to be integrated to achieve a complete picture of the inner peace discovery process. I have found that most resources focus on one of the three perspectives—

psychology, philosophy, or spirituality—while discovering inner peace requires the integration and application of pieces from all three.

For example, in Buddhist philosophy, we are told to let go of expectations, because they and our desires cause our suffering. Buddhism does not, however, address how we heal the psychological conditions, which create our desires that need to be addressed and understood before we can let these feelings go.

The following example illustrates this point. Have you ever had someone tell you to just "let it go" while you were experiencing a stressful situation? Although you cognitively understand you should let it go, you feel as though you cannot. Although "letting it go" is an important part of healing, during your emotional crisis, these words are lost because you are consumed, so to speak, by your emotional pain. You are too close. Most of us know we should let it go, but we do not know how. That is why the first step of the process is to heal those emotional scars to achieve congruency between our thoughts and feelings. It is our recurrent emotional suffering that prevents us from moving past our emotionally suffering and finding inner peace. We are missing something crucial: an understanding of why we feel the way we do. And we need this in order to gain mastery over our thoughts and feelings. If the emotional factors are not addressed, inner peace may be achieved temporarily, but it cannot be sustained for too long. If left unprocessed, negative emotions will take over at some point. You might achieve a moment of inner peace, but something such as a stressful situation could then trigger a negative feeling, destroying the newly found positive state. This is why techniques, such as meditation and yoga, are only part of the process. You may find a state of peace during meditation. However, if you have not healed your emotional scars, they are bound to resurface at a later time.

There are many people focused on spirituality who discuss "living in the now" and embracing one's spiritual side. This seems difficult to do if one is suffering emotionally. Only when we understand and process our emotions can we start to live in the moment. Emotional healing is critical to the process of discovering inner peace: we all suffer emotionally, which keeps us from feeling at peace in the first place. The point is we need to first heal those conditions that ail us before we can truly embrace the valuable teachings of philosophers and spiritualists. Only after addressing the psychological component can we guide ourselves to inner peace.

But emotional healing is only part of the journey. One can spend years exploring the past and unconscious processes, yet not truly integrate philosophical teachings or reach one's spiritual potential. It is equally important to incorporate philosophical and spiritual components into the psychological process, to guide us along the path of personal growth, and reach the ultimate goal of inner peace.

Before we go further in describing the integration of philosophy and spirituality with psychology, it is worthwhile asking ourselves: "Why don't most of us hear these messages that have been around for thousands of years?" Many of us think we know these teachings, but knowing and actually "living it" by applying it to our lives is very different. We may understand these messages intellectually, but our feelings prevent us from actually experiencing it. We also do not always understand how to apply them. Because we can't experience it, we are unaware at how profound inner peace can actually be. Furthermore, we often times doubt that we have the power to feel at peace.

One of the problems is that many philosophies do not explain why people are not hearing, understanding, and implementing the lessons, which is in part due to the psychological nature of human suffering. My belief is that change occurs when people understand why they do the things they do, feel the way they feel, and think the way they think. This is one of the basic principles of psychotherapy. The therapist and the client explore the "why" motivating a client to feel and think a certain way. And once the "why" is discovered, and the client is ready to change, he or she can start the healing process. Sometimes, just by knowing "why" can create immediate change.

Throughout this book, I will be referring to "Jane" to illustrate some of the principles in this book. Jane is a representation of many individuals I have encountered. She is not a specific client or student, but a representation of the common struggles that many of us face. Here is Jane's story.

Jane started her journey of self discovery by taking stress management classes. In addition to attending classes, she was seeing a therapist regularly. During this time, she was experiencing setbacks, primarily because she had recently moved and many things were going wrong with her new home. During one especially stressful moment, she had the opportunity to sit down, and she asked herself: "Why am I really stressed?" After much soul searching, she came to the realization that things were not working out to her satisfaction and, moreover, that this was in some way a reflection upon her. She further came to realize that what went wrong did not cause her distress; it was rather her feelings about the circumstances that were the culprit. Her constant striving for perfection, along with her feelings of inadequacy, was causing her stress. Ultimately, they were preventing her from finding inner peace.

She eventually realized the source of this perfection-seeking: feeling she could never please her parents. And if she did not receive approval, she did not feel loved. Therefore, being perfect was important, because only then did she feel she would receive love. Upon this discovery, she said she felt lighter, as if a big burden were lifted from her shoulders. This changed her life. She was able to "let go" of this feeling of perfectionism and stated that she felt less stressed. When she was able to see the "why" of and the reason for her stress, she was able to release it. She realized that this was no longer serving her. Without discovering the "why," she would have continued to be stressed by events that triggered her need to be perfect. And she would have been blocked from moving toward peace.

Many of you may have experienced similar phenomenon. When you understand the "why" of your actions, and reactions to those actions, then you will be able to do something about them. When you understand the why, then you can "let it go." Throughout this book, you will have an opportunity to explore this for yourself.

All of us have read philosophical and spiritual messages and wondered "How can I do it? How can I apply these principles of inner peace within my life?" Many of these philosophies seem to work well in theory, but individuals struggle with how to apply them to their lives. These theories are complex and lengthy, and do not provide the practical "how to" steps to implement these ideas. I hope that my book will rectify this situation and it will provide real life, step-by-step methods. My book is designed to provide a more simplified version of these theories, highlight the common elements that most of these theories share, and express how they can be practically integrated into the search for peace.

The Aim of Life is not Merely the Pursuit of Happiness, but the Discovery of Inner Peace

The aim of life is not merely the pursuit of happiness, but the discovery of inner peace. And yet many of us have not found inner peace. There are many reasons why we have not. One is that we believe that the goal of life is the pursuit of happiness. But pursuing happiness is only transient and will not lead us to inner peace. It is not that the pursuit of happiness is a bad thing, but it is very different from discovering inner peace.

Let's examine some of the inherent problems with the pursuit of happiness. Happiness is a short-lived phenomenon. We can compare happiness to a drug, because it has some similar characteristics. It allows us to escape the pain that we are feeling but, like a drug, the high wears off and we are left feeling the pain, looking for a way to avoid it. Many of us use the pursuit of happiness as a way of distracting ourselves from our pain. Most of us are in pain, and no amount of money, fame, or fortune can change or mask that.

You have probably said, "I would be happy if . . . I had a better job, made more money, lost weight, etc." Now imagine obtaining that which you think would bring you happiness. Sure, you would feel happy to some degree. However, when you do find happiness, it cannot be sustained; like any other emotion, it can only be kept going for a short time. In fact, research has been done on lottery winners. Although they experience an increase in happiness shortly after winning, within a year, they are usually feeling exactly as they did before winning.

Another way of thinking about this is to compare negative emotions to a headache. It is easy to take an aspirin (akin to the pursuit of happiness) to eliminate it, but if this headache reoccurs daily, it would be much wiser to figure out the cause of the headache. Taking an aspirin is only a band-aid and not a long-term solution. In order to truly eradicate these problems, you need to examine and process them. Analogously, the journey to find true inner peace begins by exploring the feelings that initially created the negative emotion.

Another problem with the pursuit of happiness is that we tend to search for it outside ourselves. We think that someone or something, such as a pleasurable experience, an exciting activity, or a material possession will "cure" us of our unhappiness. When we finally discover the object of our happiness, we find to our amazement and dismay that the pain does not necessarily go away.

Furthermore, what happens if you don't get the job or find a better mate? You essentially give the power to an external force that may not come through for you. Your happiness is then contingent on factors that you cannot control. Seeking happiness outside ourselves gives power over us to external factors. It is difficult to find inner peace if you do not feel in control and if you are waiting for something external to make you happy.

Additionally, the pursuit of happiness generally implies that it will be found in the future. This is problematic because it diminishes what happiness exists in the present. But part of the exploration of peace is acceptance of our current situation, which leads to finding peace despite present circumstances. You might possibly go so far as to think that the future does not even exist, and simply imagine the precious moments that you have in the present, experiences you have not heretofore been fully appreciating. Inner peace is something that you can experience right now, in the now, about the now, in spite of your current situation. With inner peace comes joy, which is different from happiness, because happiness is a judgment based on an external circumstance, something found outside of your self. Joy comes from within. It is important to first find inner peace, which can and will lead you to true happiness, rather than vice versa.

There is another stumbling block to consider. Many of us struggle to find inner peace, because many of the theories that espouse it go against popular belief. But as Oscar Wilde said, "Everything popular is wrong." For example, most of us do not believe that we create our own unhappiness. We have been taught that external things cause our pain, and only dealing with these things will bring us happiness. However, the reality is that it is our thoughts about ourselves and the world that cause us unhappiness. Furthermore, most of us have not been taught that we can control our thoughts and feelings. Nobody has ever taught you how powerful you truly are and how to tap into that inner power to find true contentment. Nobody has ever shown you a different way of living, by looking inward for the answers. Nobody has ever explained that true power is power that comes from within, not exerting power over external things. Nobody has ever emphasized just how powerful finding inner peace truly is. Nobody, until now, has taught you these valuable life lessons.

Here is something to think about: if history has ever taught us anything, it is that many of the beliefs that we hold true are often proven false. For example, at one time, we believed that the world was flat and that the sun revolved around the earth. A few individuals challenged this thinking, and eventually these beliefs were proven not to be correct. Imagine that everything you hold to be true can actually be wrong. Have you ever taken the time to examine the beliefs you have about yourself and the world? Where were those beliefs created? Are they accurate? Are they authentically yours? If you continue to live your life under a certain belief system, it will be difficult to change and grow. I encourage you to keep an open mind, challenge your beliefs and those created by society, and seek the peace that you desire.

This Book will Guide you in the Process of Discovering Inner Peace

We each experience our journey to inner peace in our own unique way. The mission of this book is to help you discover your own unique path to inner peace by examining, understanding, and integrating the components needed to facilitate this process, including certain philosophies that need to be understood and embraced to continue living at peace. This book is not intended as a quick fix. Discovering inner peace, despite what others may want you to think, is not easy and may be a life-long endeavor. However, this book can assist you in understanding part of this process. Moreover, it is not necessarily intended to be the only tool you will use during your journey.

In fact, it is highly recommended that you gather other resources to guide you on this journey, including working with a therapist and conducting additional reading, such as reading the referenced theories and books in their entirety. A therapist can also be quite helpful in your journey. He or she can help you understand the "whys" of why you think and feel the way you do and provide you with support during this process. A therapist can also help validate your feelings, and provide you with a safe place to explore and process them.

My hope is to inspire you to embark on your own journey and answer some of the questions you may have during this process, as well as, give you a taste of various philosophies that you may choose to explore more fully at a later time. However, it is important to understand that this book is intended to provide you with some tools, but the actual journey is your own unique experience. I encourage you to follow your inner wisdom, because you have the key to inner peace. This book is only a compilation of some of the things that I have learned and I encourage you to impart some of your wisdom within this process.

As you read on in this book, you might understand a concept, but find it difficult to grasp in terms of implementing it in your life. If you get to that point, you may need to take a step back and reflect inward. You may need to ask yourself: "Why is this so difficult for me?" I suggest returning to the beginning sections of this book. It may be that you need to go back to step one, healing from your past. Furthermore, the first step of healing from your past may be a difficult thing to do on your own, and I highly encourage that you seek outside help with this process. The first section, healing from the past, represents what will probably be the longest part of your journey. As events unfold in your life, you will have the opportunity to utilize some of its techniques.

Most importantly, be patient with the process. At some point, you may need to go back and re-read sections. You might even have an "aha" moment weeks later. I expect that as you read this book, your thoughts will challenge many of its words. You might think, "Well this is interesting, but I can't do it. How practical is this?" I encourage you to challenge these thoughts. Why shouldn't you be able to do this? Isn't feeling at peace important? Sometimes, when we want to change, we need to alter our whole belief system. Imagine all that you will gain from this experience. You deserve to feel at peace!

Reflection

The aim of life is not merely the pursuit of happiness, but the discovery of inner peace. We are all searching for inner peace, because we all suffer. We all experience feelings of sadness, hurt, anger, anxiety, disappointment, frustration, loneliness, restlessness, resentfulness, emptiness, and even despair, which keep us from finding inner peace. What thoughts and feelings do you have that keep you from finding inner peace?

Inner peace is not the pursuit of pleasure. It is being mentally, physically, and spiritually in a state of harmony, calm, and bliss. It is the feeling of serenity in the face of adversity. The discovery of inner peace is important, because it assists you in taking control of your life. When you achieve inner peace, this is when you have found your true power. Have you confused the pursuit of pleasure with finding inner peace? What does inner peace mean for you? How will your life be richer and fuller while discovering inner peace? List some of the benefits you hope to receive.

PSYCHOLOGICAL HEALING

As human beings we all want to be happy and free from misery. We have learned that the key to happiness is inner peace. The greatest obstacles to inner peace are disturbed emotions such as anger, attachment, fear and suspicion, while love and compassion and a sense of universal responsibility are the sources of peace and happiness.

-Dalai Lama

Most of us Live our Lives without ever Understanding our Thoughts and Emotions, but through Awareness, we can all Change How we Think and Feel

One of the most important lessons to learn is that the only things that you truly possess, and therefore control, are your thoughts and feelings. Ask yourself if you truly believe that you can control your thoughts and feelings? Even if you believe you can control your thoughts and feelings, I can assure you that there have been many times when you acted in anger, expressed another emotion in an unproductive way, or created stress for your self due to an irrational belief or misperception. These are all instances in which you were not in control of your thoughts or feelings.

Many of us think that we cannot control our thoughts or feelings, but I know that anyone can change how they think and feel. It is just that, until now, you never learned how to accomplish this. This book is focused on helping you step outside of yourself and make life-altering changes. It is time to take ownership of your thoughts and feelings, because they motivate every decision you make. And in order to take ownership, it is important to understand why you think and feel the way you do.

Most of us live our lives without ever understanding our thoughts and emotions, even though thoughts and emotions play a role in every moment of our lives and prevent us from finding inner peace. First, it is important to understand the physiology of our thoughts and feelings because, to most of us, thoughts and feelings are ambiguous things that we simply don't understand. You may have never thought how a thought or an emotion "works" and how they are created, or about their physiology. However, how can you possibly feel in control of a process if you do not really know exactly what it is? For example, if you were interested in investing money, you would learn about investments or seek counsel from someone who does.

Isn't your peace of mind worth the same investment in terms of understanding why you think and feel the way you do? Isn't your wellbeing just as precious, if not more so, than any possession you may have? Therefore, we need to gather as much information as possible, because knowledge is empowerment.

According to the Institute of Noetic Sciences, the creator of the movie *What the Bleep Do We Know*, our emotions, just like our thoughts, are created by the brain. The brain is built of tiny nerve cells called neurons. Neurons connect to other neurons and form a neural network. When neurons connect, they create a thought, which eventually imprints in our memory. The more we think the same thought, the more we reinforce this neural connection. This is a very important concept, because this explains why it is so difficult to change how we think and, consequently, how we feel, because our thoughts are actually "hard-wired" in the brain. We can think of our thoughts as habits, and to break a habit takes time and intention. If you practice stopping or changing a thought, the neural connections become weaker.

For example, say you noticed that you see life in a pessimistic way and you want to change that view. Every time you have a pessimistic thought, you need to stop it and replace it with an optimistic one. In time, you will weaken the neural pathways associated with pessimistic thinking and reinforce optimistic thinking, making the positive view more automatic. It is like learning a new dance step. When you learn the foot work to salsa, at first the steps are hard to perform. You have to learn each step separately and then consciously think about your foot work as you dance. But you reinforce the foot work by practicing until it is almost automatic. When you then hear salsa music, you do not have to consciously remember the foot work. Your feet just move to the beat. However, when you stop dancing salsa for an extended period of time, the connections in the brain weakens because you are no longer reinforcing it. When you try to dance, having quit after a significant amount of time, you will most likely need a refresher course or be more conscious of the steps, until it becomes automatic again. This is similar to how your thoughts connect.

When we interact with the environment, our brain assesses the information at hand, and our understanding is colored by past experiences. When we assess it cognitively, we then have an emotional response to what is occurring at that moment. These emotions are chemicals that are designed to imprint these thoughts into our memory. These chemicals are created in the hypothalamus which is located in the brain. The brain creates a chemical that matches every emotion that we experience. When we have an emotion, the brain assembles the chemical and then releases it into the bloodstream. There is a chemical for every emotion, such as anger, fear, jealousy, and love. Every cell in our body has thousands of receptor sites, and these chemicals attach to these receptor sites, which activates the cell and changes it. Each cell is alive and has consciousness, and it craves these chemical reactions. There are receptor sites for all emotions.

By experiencing a certain emotion regularly, our cell changes in that it creates more receptor sites for that chemical, similar to how our cells change due to psychotropic drugs, such as nicotine. We then actually become addicted to our emotional experiences. If you become angry everyday, your cells will eventually crave anger. This also explains how we get addicted to other people. We get addicted to love, for example, because we enjoy the biochemical reaction we experience, which is why we go through withdrawal when the relationship ends or we are not near them for a significant amount of time.

Because our cells are impacted by our emotional experiences, intense emotional experiences appear to damage the cells because they create an abundance of receptor cites that do not allow other important things to enter the cell, such as nutrients. This compromises our health and ages us, which is why finding inner peace is so important. It is not only vital for our emotional health, but physical health as well. This is why it is important for us not to look at our emotional and physical selves as separate. They are connected. Indeed, more and more researchers are speculating that most, if not all of our illnesses are rooted in our emotional experiences. We already know how chronic stress impacts our immune system. This is why healing our emotional scars is so important—equally important as healing our body. We cannot sustain good health if we are continually experiencing negative emotions on a daily basis. I bet you never learned this in biology class!

This is not to say that emotions are bad; emotions are necessary because they color our lives and are part of who we are. This is why avoiding our emotions is not healthy. Nor is it healthy to be overwhelmed or addicted to our emotional experiences. Rather, the healthy place to be is to experience your emotions, not by being addicted to or overwhelmed by them, nor by being afraid of or avoiding them. Now that we have demystified the process, it might be easier to get a handle of your thoughts and emotions.

Next, it is important to understand how our emotional suffering is created, because it is our emotional suffering that prevents us from finding inner peace, and it is important to understand how this process works. Most theorists agree that the experiences we encounter during our childhood create our emotional and cognitive foundation. During our developmental years, through the experiences we encounter, we react with fear, anger, sadness, disappointment, etc. These experiences shaped our perceptions of ourselves and the world around us. As children, we created fantasies about why things happen. Since we learned about ourselves and the world through these limited experiences, our understanding is not always accurate. All of these factors create inaccurate thinking.

As we grow older, we continue to use these inaccurate paradigms, which in turn distort our reality by applying past experiences to try to explain our present reality. As mentioned previously, when we encounter new information, our brain automatically compares it to information that is already stored. It is difficult for the brain to store information that is unique because it almost automatically wants to categorize it into something with which it is familiar. However, by being conscious of this, we can change the process. So, we usually do not see reality as it truly is. We use our past experiences to interpret our current reality.

This is problematic because our past experiences have nothing to do with our current reality. For example, three different people can see an accident and have three different accounts as to what happened. This happens because each person appraises their reality based on past information. If you were to think that people driving red cars are bad drivers because they speed, you may actually misperceive what happened in the accident in that you would swear that the person driving the red car was at fault, because he or she was driving too fast. Again we don't view the reality as it is, but as we perceive it to be. Our perceptions are quite faulty. When we assess our experiences, whether internal or external, we produce thoughts that then create feelings. We continue to apply our old paradigms, which recreate these feelings of fear, hate, sadness, hurt, anger, jealousy, disappointment, restfulness, and so many others. Furthermore, it is problematic, because as adults, we rarely reappraise our belief systems.

These emotions erupt from two sources: our unconscious, which is composed of unresolved emotions from past experiences; and our feelings, based on appraisals of the present. This foundation motivates all of the decisions that we make, even if we are not consciously aware of it. It also impacts how we react to and feel about our current experiences, as well as, what we think and feel about ourselves and about others. These emotional scars create current pain because present circumstances trigger the feelings that hurt so much. Furthermore, even if we don't feel that we have been scarred during our childhood, we are still stressed by inaccurate or irrational beliefs that were created during our formative years. This is why we continually experience pain and do not feel at peace. Moreover, this contributes to depression, anxiety, addictions, and other psychological ailments.

For example, this is why interaction with family members can be so emotional. Let's take a look at Jane. When she goes home for the holidays, she always gets upset with her parents when they make critical comments. The reason she feels hurt is that, during her childhood, she felt as though she never received her parents' approval, an old scar that re-currently triggers pain throughout her life. Furthermore, she has an unconscious desire for her parents to approve of her and not be critical. She does not realize that her parents' criticism is not a lack of approval. Even though her parents are critical, they love her very much. Her parents are simply critical people.

However, Jane does not understand this dynamic and is made continually upset by it. She does not understand that her parents probably won't change, something she desires very much, leading to hurt. Furthermore, because she believes that her parents are critical, she may misinterpret their and potentially others' comments as being critical. Based on her past experiences and the thought pattern she has created, she believes that others are critical of her. This then validates her beliefs that others are critical and it in some respect becomes a self-fulfilling prophecy, because she will be looking out for criticism in others. Whenever Jane does not get approval from others, she is upset because this also triggers an unconscious desire for approval.

Jane becomes emotionally stuck and continues to live her life trying to satisfy these needs. Because she never felt she received approval, she will continue to seek it, and feel pain if it is not received. It is only when she discovers that seeking approval is not serving her, and only causing her pain, that she can change. If Jane embarks on the journey of healing from her past, she will come to understand this dynamic and, next year, during the holidays, her parents' comments might not have an emotional effect on her. Most of us can relate to her experience.

We carry all of these emotional scars and dysfunctional thinking into our present and, until they are made conscious, addressed, and processed, they impact every moment of our lives and motivate our decisions. Have you ever wondered why you feel and think the way that you do? Most of the decisions that we make are predicated on thoughts and feelings that in turn stem from these conscious and unconscious processes that we created long ago. We carry these cognitive and emotional blueprints into our adult life and, if not examined, they stifle our ability to live fully and prevent us from finding peace. How we have viewed our situations in the past colors how we view situations in the present. We are not seeing things as they truly are. This creates emotional pain. Although difficult to believe, we are still emotionally operating exactly the same way we did when we were children. We come into current reality with preconceived notions and react in certain ways that are no longer serving us. The factors that influence our emotional reactions include what we experienced, how we coped with our situation, what support we received, how we interpreted these situations and so much more. If our emotional scars are not healed, they will continue to affect us, preventing us from finding inner peace.

Therefore, the first step in discovering inner peace is to heal from the past. This requires us to examine and understand the past and how it impacts us presently. Healing also calls for us to process the feelings that create our suffering and let them go. It means accepting our past and forgiving all those who have hurt us. Healing also means gaining mastery over our thoughts and feelings in the present. All of these actions will be discussed in the first section of this book.

Healing from your past may be the longest part of your journey, because there are so many different layers that comprise our cognitive and emotional selves. This journey consists of a number of steps, including self-reflection, validation of your emotions, feeling your feelings, and challenging your beliefs and perceptions.

What Keeps us from Exploring the Past

Before we discuss self-exploration, it is useful to know and understand some of the barriers that stand in its way. We all, in some form or another, defend against negative feelings. One of the barriers that prevent us from exploring the past is that, despite copious research proving as much, people do not truly believe that their past has anything to do with their present. Most researchers agree that your past has everything to do with your present.

To help illustrate this point, let's look at how we handle stress. It is important to understand that each of us reacts and deals with situations in different ways. One can conclude, moreover, that it is possible that the way one deals with situations is based on individual past experiences. In fact, the event is not the problem, per se; the issue is rather how we perceive and react to it. Events are emotionally neutral in nature. However, each of us attaches meaning to current events, which can cause distress. This is the basic premise of cognitive behavioral theory. Therefore, if we can change how we think about our present, we can change how we feel.

So, why is it that we react to stress differently? Isn't it logical to assume that past experiences color how we view situations? Why then do we so often disregard this fact?

Let's take a common situation to which we can all relate. You get an email from your boss who wants to meet with you. Do we all react in the same way? Of course not: some of us get nervous and automatically jump to the worst-case scenario. We may wonder what we did wrong. We may spend a sleepless night thinking of all the possible negative scenarios. However, some of us may think in a more positive way. We may wonder if we are getting a promotion or a raise. The stress is not in the email from the boss, but the meaning we attach to it.

Why is it that in the same situation, different people will react in different ways? It is because our perceptions of current situations are usually based on past experiences, and not necessarily on our current reality. Some of us fear figures of authority because we feared our parents. Some have either optimistic or pessimistic views based on past experiences. Again, we interpret our present by our past experiences. There is considerable research showing how our past experiences, if not addressed, dictate our present. This manifests itself in how we cope with stressors, and even how we choose our mates. We are also sensitive to interactions with family members, because these interactions trigger the hurt from our past. These are ways that show how our past has a profound effect on our present.

Isn't it logical to assume that our thoughts and feelings have something to do with our past? I bet if you look at how you react to certain situations, you will realize that you have always reacted to them in a similar way. Therefore, it is important to understand how you react to situations. It is also important to go one step further, not only identifying the thoughts and feelings, but also getting to the origin of these thoughts and feelings. Because once you understand the "why" in why you feel things, it is so much easier to understand how to change.

Another barrier to examining our past is that thoughts about our past are painful. Our consequent feelings about our experiences are painful for many different reasons. We do not talk about our emotions, so they are ambiguous and sometimes scary. Because we don't understand our emotions, it feels as if we cannot control them, and they appear to have considerable power over us. However, it is important that you understand the physiology behind your thoughts and feelings, as explained earlier, in order to best put them in perspective. Remember, emotions are merely brain chemicals that set perceptions in long-term memory. When we start to understand this process and learn to cope with our feelings, the pain will subside.

Our feelings are also painful because, during our developmental years, they are frequently invalidated, making them even more misunderstood. That can make us feel ashamed about our emotion experiences. These invalidated feelings prevent us from learning how to cope with our emotional pain. Because we cannot cope with our emotions, they either overwhelm us or, because our feelings are uncomfortable, we try to avoid them. Our inability to deal effectively with emotions compromises our self-esteem, which can lead us to feel hopeless. Some may even become so overwhelmed by the pain that they feel their only option is to end their lives. Others spend most of their lives trying to avoid their emotions, thereby not living fully. Because we either try to prevent feelings from overwhelming us, or work to avoid our feelings, we tend to use maladaptive coping mechanisms. However, by understanding our emotions, what will hopefully occur is that we will take charge of our emotions, rather than have our emotions control us.

Another reason why our emotions are so painful, especially during childhood, is that like food and shelter, we needed love and nurturing to thrive. We all know that babies, despite being given sustenance such as food and water, will not survive if not given love. This is why any thwarting of this process can create emotional scars during childhood. No matter how small they may seem to us as adults, these emotional conflicts can be incredibly painful for children, because they are so important to their survival. We sometimes recognize this pain, at least partially, or we push it into our subconscious because it makes us feel uncomfortable, painful, and vulnerable. Although we all differ in terms of the types of experiences we encountered, we all feel the resulting emotional scars that prevent us from finding peace. That is why it is important to work through the pain. Though emotional pain hurts us, no matter how terrible, it will not kill us. By continually working on it and through it, you can learn not to fear your emotional pain.

Fear is a tremendous barrier to self-examination. One of our primary fears is that, if we explore ourselves, we might realize that something is wrong with us. And generally, we think it is best to deny that this might be true. However, if you had a recurrent headache, wouldn't you want to discover the root of the problem to prevent it from recurring? Why is it that we treat emotional pain differently? Because our emotional self is probably the most personal to us, it is highly vulnerable to scrutiny. The idea that "I am not emotionally okay" has, in some ways, been misconstrued to mean, "I am not okay." This is because it is difficult to separate our feelings from who we are. But it is important to realize you are not your feelings or your thoughts. Your feelings and thoughts are just a part of who you are. There does not have to be a stigma attached to exploring these feelings. Again, because our emotions are merely chemical interactions in the brain, addressing it should be no different from addressing a headache. Therefore, it is important to put our emotional wellbeing in perspective and deal with it just as we would deal with any physical ailment. As we know, emotional distress will eventually lead to physical distress.

We also fear the discovery of a dysfunctional childhood would reflect poorly upon us. However, you are separate from your childhood experiences in that, no matter what has happened, you are not the sum of your experiences. You are wonderful and special. Some of us feel ashamed regarding our childhood experiences. We have to remember, though, we did not choose our past. When we were children, we were, to some extent, victims of our situation because we were unable to make the choices that we can make as adults. We also did not learn the tools we needed to cope with situations. At any moment, you can choose not to continue being the victim of your past and change how you think, feel, and act. Your past does not define who you are. You are who you choose to be in the present and you can decide who you want to be in the future. Your past experiences do not have anything to do with your present unless you allow them.

Your past is useful in understanding why you think, act, and feel the way you do because it influences your thoughts and feelings, which you can change once you understand the process. For example, you may believe that you are vulnerable and need to protect yourself from others because, in your past, others harmed you. However, just because people have hurt you in the past does not mean that you are bad or weak, whatever you might feel. This also means that in your present people do not have to hurt you. There are malicious people, but you no longer need to feel vulnerable as an adult because you have tools to protect you. As you will see, you can learn how not to experience hurt when other's wrong you.

Being overly protective of yourself does not allow you to live freely. However, sometimes due to the beliefs that we have, they become self-fulfilling prophecies, which is why it is so important to not bring old paradigms into your current thinking. To further lessen this fear, it is important to understand that we all share the same journey. We have all been scarred by the past. This is what we all share. Our past creates emotional scars, and personal growth is the process of uncovering and healing those scars. Self-improvement should not be viewed in a punitive way.

Another fear that prevents us from self-reflection is that we are frightened we might be "crazy" or "mentally ill." Our lack of knowledge about our emotional lives, as well as, the fear instilled by the media, is another factor that propagates this fear. It is interesting that, in our society, we do not have a problem going to a doctor if we have an ailment, but we feel that we need to struggle alone with our emotional needs. It may be that we do not view our physical health as personally. It is as if having diabetes is not as personal as feeling depression. It could be that physical ailments are viewed differently from psychological ailments because we are not taught to believe that everyone suffers and that our emotions are purely biochemical reactions.

Instead, we fear being labeled as "crazy," "insane," or "mentally ill." There is this confusion that, if I am feeling sad or anxious, I may be "crazy," and only "crazy" people seek therapy and explore their feelings. Currently, mental health practitioners label people as "mentally ill," but true insanity is having a "brain disease," which only affects a very small population. "Being crazy" is when someone has an organic brain disease that prevents them from being in touch with reality and can manifest itself, for example, in hallucinations and delusions. Therapy cannot help brain disease. Therapy and personal growth work is intended for "sane" people. Much more likely in being human is to have feelings such as depression and anxiety. This is not insanity. We all need help with these feelings, because all of us struggle with them, and we are all recovering, so to speak, from the scars of childhood. Isn't it time that we developed an understanding of our emotional selves and de-mystified the emotional experience?

Sometimes we confuse exploring the past with blaming the past, which can also prevent someone from self-exploration. The process of exploration is not to blame the past, but to understand what happened in the past. So often people say, "Therapists just blame all the problems on the past." This is not the case. Self-exploration is a way of understanding how our past has influenced us. This is not to say that we are victims of our past. But if not explored, our past does influence how we experience our present. Only by not looking at our past can we become victims of it, because the victim is one who allows the past to influence his or her life.

Some people believe that feeling emotions makes them "weak," which would also prevent self-exploration because it uncovers emotions. Others may think that leaving the past behind enables one to be strong. One of the reasons that we think feeling emotions is a sign of weakness is that we don't understand them, which is why our emotions have been painful in the past. Emotions are part of who we are and it is important to develop control of this process. We might also think that feeling emotions is a sign of weakness because we have seen others displaying emotions in an inappropriate way and perceive them as being unstable. Furthermore, when you are honest with how you feel, some may perceive this as vulnerability because one can get hurt if rejected by someone else after disclosing one's true feelings.

However, it is important to remember that feeling your emotions is not being overwhelmed by your emotions and that others do not necessarily prey on you if you are displaying emotions. Not allowing others to hurt you, which will be discussed later, is true strength. By choosing to avoid your emotions, by stuffing them inside, because you are afraid of them, is really not much different from an overt over-emotional display. It is just the opposite end of the same spectrum. These emotions will eventually surface at a later time, usually in anger. Therefore, the healthiest and strongest place is to feel your feelings in a healthy way. As we will discuss later, even if you are rejected by someone, this does not have to be a painful experience. It takes a strong person to be able to go back and look at the past and one's self honestly. Being weak is being ruled by our emotions, which happens if we do not develop an understanding of them. We all feel hurt, sad, disappointed, and vulnerable and just because we have these feelings does not mean we are not strong and secure. Having feelings is the nature of being human.

There are also cultural implications that may prevent self-reflection. Our western world is a highly extroverted society, whereby we spend significant attention on external factors and little time looking inward. In our Western culture, being extroverted is praised, and being an introvert is often misunderstood. Extroversion and introversion are temperaments that we are born with, and are neither good nor bad. However, introverts are often misconstrued as being shy and antisocial, which is not at all the case. What makes an introvert different from an extrovert is that introverts get their energy from within, not from external sources as extrovert do. When an introvert is tired, he or she needs to retreat in solitude to recharge, whereas an extrovert gains his energy from external sources and will need to spend time with people to recharge. An introvert is also more interested in his own internal life and naturally is more comfortable with self reflection than is the case with an extrovert. Introverts have the natural ability to look inside themselves. Because we value extroversion, introspection, which is more of a skill that comes natural to introverts, is not as valued. However, it is important for extroverts to spend some time retreating within and learning this valuable skill.

In our society, we spend considerable time on intellectual pursuits, while our emotional self is rarely addressed. It is as if our emotional self is not always viewed as important. However, if emotions are part of who we are, neglecting them is similar to neglecting a body part or neglecting intellectual pursuits. Our emotional life is equally important as anything else in our lives. Talking about and understanding our feelings are things that we simply do not really often do. This process may be uncomfortable for you precisely because we do not have experience dealing with emotions. But like any skill, as you practice, it will become more comfortable. Now that you have explored some of the barriers to self-reflection, you may want to take some time to think about how you might be blocked from reflecting upon your own self.

Step 1: Self-Reflection

An unexamined life is not worth living.

–Socrates

Most of us tend to seek answers to our problems outside of ourselves, because we have been taught that is where to find them. It is also due to the lack of confidence in our selves, as if the external world is more wise and powerful. Most of us believe that external factors influence how we think and feel. It is in fact the external factors that often actually create our misery. As mentioned above, we think of peace and happiness existing outside ourselves, leading us to think that is where we will find the answers to our questions. Yet this usually leads to unhappiness, disappointment, and frustration. As we struggle with our pain, we often try to find "external bandages," so to speak, to remedy our suffering, yet these do not fix the suffering, only suppress it for a while. This can lead to addictions. If you are feeling anxious, a drug, such as alcohol, might temporarily alleviate the anxiety. After the high wears off, anxiety is still there, or it returns soon after. To truly heal the pain, it is important to understand where that pain came from and treat it at its source. This answer can only be found within yourself.

At some point, many people learn that the journey of healing is not an external one, but an internal one. This shift in perspective can happen after gaining awareness of one's emotional suffering, after one has a life-altering experience, or when one becomes unsatisfied with the answers from outside of one's self. The experiences can lead one to pause and take a different approach. It is not that the external world isn't helpful to the process of self-enlightenment. In fact, it is quite helpful, because sometimes it is hard to explore our inner world by ourselves. We tend to look at ourselves through the colored lenses that we have always worn. Sometimes, an outsider's perspective, assuming there is no ulterior motive on their part, can be quite valuable in looking at our self objectively. This is why people find resources such as therapy to be helpful. However, the first step has to be done by you: by looking inward, even if you choose to share these experiences and gather resources from the outside.

The first step in discovering inner peace is to heal from our past. This healing consists of several steps, including: self-reflection, validating your emotions, feeling your feelings, and challenging your beliefs and perceptions.

The first action necessary to heal from our past is starting the process of self-reflection. You may wonder, "Why is self reflection important?" There are many reasons. Although it is human nature to want to find a quick fix, it is best to get to the root of the problem. We cannot truly fix a problem without really understanding its nature. We need to understand the "why" of why we think, feel, and do the things we do to fully understand how we can change them. If you feel sadness, loneliness, or anxiety, it is helpful to understand the root, and the why, of these feelings. How can you possibly heal from pain if you don't know where it came from in the first place?

For example, Jane struggles with feelings of anxiety when she is relaxing, and finds it difficult to actually find relaxation, because she has a list of things to do that is a mile long. She also notices during these periods that she always begins to reach a point of burnout, finding it hard to steer clear of collapse through relaxation. After exploring this anxiety by asking why she feels anxious, she comes to realize that she feels as if she needs to be doing something because accomplishing something validates her existence. As she thinks back to her childhood, she remembers her mother yelling at her for "doing nothing." She remembers her mother telling her that it is important to be productive and being lazy is bad. This is the origin of her anxiety because, when she is not productive, she feels inadequate. She needs to first understand the "why" behind her anxiety before she can proceed to change it.

Have you ever felt sad, angry, anxious, hurt, or lonely, with no apparent reason for the feeling, or felt that your thoughts and emotions seemed to control you? Self-reflection is important because it facilitates conscious awareness of our feelings and thoughts. Most of us are living a life in which we are not consciously aware of our emotional mind. We react to situations, as well as our feelings, without understanding why we do so. There is always a reason why we think and feel the way we do; it just may be that we have not discovered it yet. We seem to think that we have power over our lives. However, we tend to overlook the power of our thoughts and feelings, which are partially controlled by unconscious processes. The more introspection you have into this dynamic, the more power you will have over your thoughts, feelings, and actions. If you do not understand this process, you are not likely in complete control of it. Hence, you do not have control over your life. Once you become consciously aware of this process, you can live a more intentional life by making decisions that are based on intentional motivation, not satisfying needs from the past, which you do not fully understand and which are no longer serving you. Conscious living, so to speak, puts you in the driver's seat of your life. The first step in taking charge of your thoughts and feelings, and ultimately your life, is to understand this process, and not allow unconscious motivators, thoughts, and feelings to have power over you.

Self-reflection is a way to examine the past in a more enlightened state. Without it, you cannot proceed with the other steps needed for emotional healing and the discovery of inner peace. We are all scarred by our pasts and these scars impact our present. It is important to examine the past, with adult eyes, to gain a better understanding of why we think and feel the way we do. This will help uncover the root of our suffering. Often, we are so entrenched in our situation that our pain is continually perpetuated. It is important to step outside of our selves to truly see what is happening. This allows us to develop an understanding of our internal and unconscious motivators and the conflicts that lie within all of us: our desires, dreams, fears, and wishes.

You can now start the process of change by identifying the origins of your suffering. This process starts by being more conscious of your true feelings and thoughts, and taking a good hard look at yourself, truly and honestly, to assess how and why you feel the way you do, and how and why you have the thoughts that you have. Once you become more conscious of your thoughts and feelings, you are able to relate them back to their origins. By re-examining one's own past, one can see how it has shaped one's present. It is important to find that link to the past that explains why you feel and think the way that you do in the present.

As you explore your thoughts and feelings, it is important that you get clarity as to what are thoughts and what are feelings because many of us confuse thoughts for feelings or feelings for thoughts. For example, Jane made plans with a friend and her friend called to cancel their lunch date. Jane was sad and identified the following: I feel that others do not like me and I am sad. However, to begin exploring this she needs to first reframe this idea. She thinks, not feels, that others do not like her. This causes her to feel, not be, sad. It is important that she makes this distinction because she can change a thought, such as "others don't like me." Feelings are not as easy to change. When she is able to change this thought, she can then work to change her feelings.

Keep in mind that sometimes identifying the thoughts that trigger an emotional response can be difficult because sometimes our natural reaction is to deny or avoid them, or they happen so quickly and automatically that we are not aware of them. Identifying our feelings can be difficult as well because our feelings can be ambiguous or we may feel many different things. However, the more you practice, the easier it will be.

One of the things to keep in mind is that when you begin looking at your past, it is important that you approach it with self-love and forgiveness. If you are judgmental and beat yourself up with the process, your tendency will be to avoid it. Being judgmental how you think, feel, and act or have acted is not productive in any way. Your job is to be the observer, not be critical of what happened or how you think and feel about it. There are many different techniques for reflection, and this book will provide you with a few to help you get started on this journey.

An exercise that can start the process is to begin examining the things that cause you stress and how you handle them. You may want to journal your stressors and indicate what causes you to feel stress. You can reflect on the stressors of your day and write about the thoughts and feelings you experienced and how you reacted to the stressor. Once you keep a stress journal for a while, you will start to notice themes. These themes are significant in understanding what is causing you pain and suffering. After journaling these experiences, you will want to look at the origin of these thoughts and feelings.

For example, Jane noticed that she becomes stressed when she attempts to do something and it does not turn out as well as she would have wanted. When she looked at her thoughts, she realized that she gets stressed, mad, sad, and anxious when she feels that she is not perfect or not doing things perfectly.

After looking at the thoughts, it is important to understand where they originated. It is important that when a situation occurs and you feel stressed, you stop, pause, and examine it. Ask yourself: What emotional scar is this situation triggering? In the case of our student, Jane, believes that in order to be loved and receive approval from others, she needs to be perfect. If she is not, this creates distress. Her unhappiness was created because she did not feel she received approval from her parents. She also felt that, in order to be loved, she had to be perfect. She thought that the only time she felt as if she received love and approval was after she did something to earn it. She can learn to be at peace knowing that she is imperfect and realizing that her striving for perfection is exhausting. She can believe that she is special even if she is not perfect and that she is no longer the little girl that desires approval.

Another self-reflective exercise you can use is to examine a current obstacle that you might be facing and ask, "What feelings is this situation triggering in me?" and "What is there about me that I need to learn?" We can explore the obstacles that come into our lives to learn about valuable aspects of ourselves. This is a very important point to understand. As mentioned above, it is not the external factors that cause us pain, but the thoughts and the feelings these external factors triggers in us. No one or nothing can make us think or feel something. These situations only trigger feelings that are already there, conscious or unconscious, which is why, as you continue the process of personal growth, it is imperative that you continually look within yourself when you think or feel something negative. We cannot blame others or the situations we are in for our unhappiness, which is something we all usually do. It is important that as we continue this process, we start to own our thoughts and feels.

When a negative feeling arises, the first step is to get clear on the associated thought and feeling. When you have identified a specific thought and feeling, you can ask yourself, "Where did I feel this before?" or "Why is this situation making me think and feel (how I do)." Therefore, it is important to start looking for the process that is occurring within, instead of focusing on the external event and blaming it for causing us to feel a certain way. External situations such as other people, jobs, etc. cannot cause us to feel a certain way. These external factors merely trigger feelings within us that need to be explored. The thoughts and the feelings that we have are our own, they are not created by an outside source.

Going back to our example of Jane, during that time of her life, Jane was struggling with her boss. He was very authoritarian and demanding. Often, he would get angry with her because he did not feel that she was doing what he asked. Although she felt that she was doing the best that she could, any time he would offer her some constructive criticism, she would become very upset. A few times, she even found herself crying at her desk. Jane asked herself,

"Where did I feel this before?" She also asked herself, "Why is this situation making me feel upset." She came to realize that she was upset because she did not think as if she could meet his demands, which reminded her of being unable to please her authoritarian father. Her boss elicited feelings of sadness and inadequacy in her, as her father had done in her childhood. She did not realize that this was a carbon copy of her behavior regarding not being able to please her father. Importantly, she was able to establish a link between a current situation and one from her past. With some insight, she can learn that criticism is okay and it does not have to elicit an emotional response.

As you continue the process of self-reflection, it is important to continue examining the link between past and current situations. This can be difficult to do. However, when we look back on those events that scarred us in our past, we can start identifying some of the associated unconscious fears, desires, and wishes. For example, is your unconscious wish to "fix" your mother or father because they themselves were unhappy? Is that why you pick partners who are similar to them, and do you want to fix those partners? Do you expect them to change and become upset when they don't? Or is your desire to have someone come in and rescue you because you were hurt by your parent's abuse and wished that someone would just get you out of that situation? Do you wish that through other people, the circumstances that you are or have been in and the state of the world were different? The answers to these questions are so important in uncovering these unconscious processes. Once we start uncovering these processes, the next time we feel sad, hurt, rejected, disappointed, or any feeling, we can understand that it is not the current reality, but the feelings from long ago that have not been addressed.

Jane came to realize that her unconscious desire was to be rescued, because she had always wanted to be rescued as a child. This is what she expected from her relationships, that the men in her life were supposed to rescue her from her pain. She also had an unconscious desire to feel special because she never felt special as a child. This only created disappointment, because no man was ever able to provide her with the things that she thought she needed. She would continually test the men in her life, and nothing they did was good enough, because it did not satisfy her need to feel special. She would have many conflicts within the relationships she had with men since she felt they were unable to help her feel special. After several failed relationships, she was able make a connection between her present needs and the things she needed during her childhood. When she makes this connection, she can decide if she wants to continue operating in the same way.

Another avenue to explore is how we attach meaning to things that often cause us emotional pain. Jane attaches a significant amount of meaning to her appearance; regarding her weight in particular. Even the idea of gaining a minimal amount of weight is unbearable. This is directly linked to her fear of not being perfect. Others attach meaning to being liked and pleasing people, and are very upset if someone dislikes them or talks badly about them. It is important to look at what you attach meaning to in order to determine where your emotional energy is spent. You need to ask yourself, Why is this so important? And, is this something that I can let go? Often, we don't know why things are so meaningful to us, and this is why it is so important to uncover their meaning. Jane created this fantasy that others would only like her if she were perfect, and to her being thin and attractive was a sign of perfection. This is why it was meaningful to her. What things are meaningful to you that create negative feelings such as frustration and anger?

How we view ourselves also has to do with the fact that, during our formative years, we create a life script. It is important to examine this life script because, frequently, we create an image of our selves or a role that we decide to play. We play this role repeatedly throughout our lifetime. This image about our self is usually inaccurate, as it grows out of experiences from our past, not our present. This role can lead us to feel unhappy, frustrated, resentful, and so many other different feelings, since we are not being authentic to ourselves. Are you still feeling like that awkward child who did not fit in, or who felt inadequate? Or are you the helpless person who feels like a victim? Or is your role to play the caretaker or the people pleaser? Often, this role is not productive, and it causes us stress and unhappiness. It prevents us from doing the things we want to do, keeps us from being authentic, and creates pain and suffering.

By first identifying this life script, we can start re-writing it because, as we grow, this script usually doesn't serve us in a positive way. When we start to uncover these processes, we can start becoming the author of our own lives. We can, as adults, decide who we are and how we choose to live our lives. Jane came to realize that she did not like her job, but had chosen it because it was the practical thing to do. She realized that she has many artistic talents that are not being expressed, because growing up she saw herself as the practical older child and this was reinforced by her family and the messages she would receive from others. This child was to grow up and be successful, which was reflected in monetary ways. She realized that this was not who she was authentically, but continued this role as a way of trying to gain approval from her parents.

What is your life script? What role do you play? Why do you think you play this role? How can you re-write this script so that it is authentically you?

Another exercise that is helpful in understanding some of the themes of our suffering is to think about a memory that triggers a negative emotion. These memories have the keys to uncovering the themes that cause us pain. Some of us remember more events than others. However, even if you don't remember much, identifying a few early memories is very helpful. Jane recalled a vivid memory at age 7. She remembered receiving a gift: a dress from her grandmother. She remembered how much she loved the dress, because it was so beautiful. It was lavender, her favorite color, and was made of taffeta with iridescent ruffles. She recalled that her mother noticed a tear in the dress. They rushed to the store to exchange it, but to her horror, they did not have a replacement. She can still remember the disappointment she felt. She learned that it is painful when she did not get what she wanted and that life is unfair; she believed that she deserved this dress, but it was torn and there was no replacement. This dress represents the continual disappointment that she felt throughout her childhood and life, which triggers this particular pain any time she is disappointed. Whenever she is disappointed, she feels like that little sad girl who cannot have her beautiful dress. Jane would continually expect that she would be disappointed and, therefore, was very demanding and unhappy. Can you recall any such memories that significantly shaped your life?

Understanding the feelings that result from the dynamics in relationships can also lead you to understand your scars from the past. We often chose relationships with others to resolve psychological conflicts from the past. We pick significant others that in some way resemble our parents, or other significant persons from our past, because we have unresolved unconscious desires and needs. We are attracted to these others because the dynamic feels familiar. Moreover, we want to emotionally "fix" the things we were unable to fix in our past. Because we did not satisfy an emotional need that was established in our earlier years, we try to get it from our partners. But this only leaves us frustrated, hurt, and disappointed when it invariably is not met.

We also find it difficult to leave dysfunctional relationships, because we have this psychological need that has not been met. This dynamic prevents us from having healthy relationships and picking healthy partners, and from accepting our partners for who they are. This explains why we are always looking to change our mates, and are so often hurt by the things they do or do not do.

Jane's parents were emotionally distant, and her desire was to feel close to them. She found herself choosing significant others who were also distant and she consequently became hurt and frustrated when they exhibited this trait. Her desire was to change them, because that was the fantasy from her childhood. She simply wanted her parents to be emotionally available. Jane was continually disappointed, because they would not change, and she found it difficult to leave these relationships, clinging to the desire for them to be different. If they changed, this would satisfy her psychological need for wanting her parents to change. Once she understood this process, she could start to choose partners who are emotionally healthier and more available, understanding that her process of picking partners was largely due to this unconscious process, which is no longer necessary for her.

Whatever the feeling—sadness, anger, hurt, or anxiety—it is important to get to the root of the feeling and the thought. Have you ever had an experience when you logically knew something, but you felt a different way about the circumstance? This feeling, which often times overrides logic, stems from somewhere, and it is important for you to get to the bottom of it. That is why it is important to explore these feelings. They can be quite powerful.

This process of self-exploration will help align your logical with your emotional mind. The process will allow you to live both logically and emotionally, living fully by feeling your feelings, and not avoiding them or being overwhelmed by them. As mentioned, it is important to explore the past, not deny it. Many of us think we are strong because we have put the past behind us, but we are not necessarily any stronger than those who lament about their pasts. It does take strong person to be able to look at oneself honestly. We all feel hurt, sad, disappointed, or vulnerable. Just because we have these feelings does not mean we are not strong and secure. Having feelings is the nature of being human. It is the truly strong person who can feel and examine these feelings. It is important to understand that, although we were largely powerless regarding the events that molded us, we are powerful enough to make changes to how we think and feel in the present. Once you are conscious of this process, you will uncover many things that are preventing you from finding peace.

Step 2: Validating your Emotions

Cherish your own emotions and never unvalued them
–Robert Henri

Once you have explored your past, and discovered how your past has created the feelings of hurt, anger, sadness, frustration, etc. that impact you today, it is important to validate those feelings.

Our emotions are so painful precisely because they were not validated very often during our developmental years. When our emotions are not validated, we don't learn how to cope with them effectively, and we have a tendency to try to rationalize or avoid them. Our emotions are painful because we have not learned how to soothe ourselves. We then also neglect our emotions and, as mentioned above, they can overwhelm and control us.

Do you remember what a terrible feeling it was when you felt something very strongly and then, when you shared it with someone else, they told you, "It's not that bad. Get over it." When your feelings are not validated, it feels as if they do not matter. And that can make you feel as if you do not matter. If our emotions are not validated at an early age, they create a sense of shame regarding our emotional state, and we feel misunderstood, all of which impacts our present self-esteem.

When we look back at our past, we use rationalization because we are looking at these events through our current "adult" eyes. Furthermore, we do not even always look at our childhood experiences and, when we do, we generally minimize them. Sometimes, we don't even recall many of them.

To start the validation process, it is important to try to look at these feelings as if you were that child, looking at them in present time. Sometimes, when we consider our past, we think "It wasn't that bad," or "It's understandable why things happened the way they did," or "My parents treated me the way they did because of the circumstances that they were having." But we also think, "It's in the past, and there is nothing I can do about it." However, in order to proceed to the next step, which is to feel our feelings, it is important that you validate the feelings you had regarding those events.

Think back as the child that you were and examine how you truly felt, and what you really thought about these experiences. Examine how painful, traumatic, dangerous, even unstable the situations really were. How did these experiences mold your emotional experiences? How did these experiences shape how you see yourself and your world?

As adults, we can validate our own emotional experiences, even if they were not validated before. We can validate these feelings, after we have identified them, by saying to ourselves, "It was okay to be sad (or hurt, angry, disappointed, etc.—be very specific with the feeling.). It was understandable that during that time I was feeling sad (hurt, angry, etc.)." Imagine yourself as a child reliving these experiences to really identify how painful they were. Sometimes it is difficult for us to validate our own feelings, which is why some seek outside help. This is one of the most powerful processes that happens in therapy and why most people feel good when they talk to a therapist. The therapist does not judge one's feelings, but validates them. External validation is a very powerful tool in the healing process. So, if you are struggling to validate your own feelings, find someone who can help you.

Step 3: Feeling your Feelings, and Starting to Let Them Go

The best and most beautiful things in the world cannot be seen, nor touched, but are felt in the heart.

-Hellen Keller

Once you have identified the origins of your pain and validated your feelings, the next step is to feel those feelings—truly feel them. When negative emotions are experienced, we tend to push them away because we are either afraid to feel them or they are too painful. You need to understand that, at some point, those emotions will surface in some form or another. Sometimes, we try to avoid feeling hurt, but when we try to suppress the emotions, they can manifest at a later time as anger. We have all experienced a situation whereby someone or something upsets us, but we don't fully feel the feelings, and later on we might get angry with someone who really was not the intended target of our anger, almost automatically.

As you work on your exercise of exploring the past, it is important that you sit with these feelings and truly feel them. When you start to feel your feelings, feel them with the understanding that soon you will them go. They do not have to be overwhelming, because you can control the process now that you know what you are dealing with. Feel the sadness, feel the anger, feel all the pain and, once you do, only then should you start to let those feelings go. When you feel these feelings, do not judge them, and do not judge yourself. Try not to allow your rational mind to stop this process. If these feelings overwhelm you, keep in mind that you are in control of these feelings, and you are choosing to truly feel them because you know that, in order to overcome them, you must first truly experience them.

After you have spent some time truly feeling your feelings, then you must ask yourself important questions: are these feelings valid, useful, or serving any purpose; or are your feelings causing you to feel sad, angry, anxious, or non-productive? Hopefully, you come to the realization that these feelings are not serving you and are preventing you from living a full life. Most, if not all, of our negative emotions are not serving us in a positive way. We can make the choice to let them go. We can also better let them go when we realize that the current pain we are feeling stems from negative emotions created in our past. It is usually when we get to the origin of the pain can we truly let it go. They are not serving us in our present, because they prevent us from truly being happy and at peace. If, after this process, you are still having difficulty letting these feelings go, you may need to re-explore the matter.

Jane was having difficulty letting go of the anger she felt regarding how critical her parents were during her childhood. She realized that she was still unable to let go of the anger and she continued to feel angry when they would make critical remarks. She wanted to let it go, but could not. Upon further examination, she came to an important realization: she believed that if she were not angry, it was as though she were condoning this behavior. She would come to realize that her anger was only hurting her, and that not being angry did not mean that she agreed with her parents' behavior.

She also felt that, by being angry, she became her parents' punisher. With time, she discovered that her anger was only punishing her. There was no way to truly punish them. Furthermore, she also realized that she had this unconscious desire that they would change and, post-criticism, she would feel accepted and loved. Therefore, some of this anger was due to her frustration that they were not changing. She would eventually come to realize that her parents are critical for their own reasons, and they would probably not change. She also realized that this did not mean that she was not loved.

Step 4: Challenging Dysfunctional Beliefs and Perceptions

The first and the best victory is to conquer self.

-Plato

Once we examine our past, validate our emotions, and feel our feelings, we can start to challenge our dysfunctional beliefs and perceptions. This also helps us let go of negative emotions. It is important to identify the beliefs we have about ourselves and about others, as well as, about our desires and needs, because these beliefs continually re-create negative emotions.

Our beliefs seem to us to serve an important purpose, and we are not always inclined to want to think they are dysfunctional. However, if a belief leads you to feel a negative emotion, it is definitely worth exploring. On some level, it is dysfunctional. Challenging our beliefs can be a difficult thing to do because many of the beliefs we have are long and deeply held. We usually think we are our thoughts and they are us, because they are a part of who we have become. This challenges our belief system, becoming a threat to our self-esteem. It is important to understand a few things. Most of our beliefs were formed through childhood experiences. But these were not completely accurate.

It is important to understand that our thoughts and beliefs are not who we are. This idea may surprise you. But think back to a time when you changed a thought. We do it all the time. But who is doing the changing? If we presume that we are our thoughts, we would not be able to change them. So keep in mind, our thoughts are only a part of us.

These thoughts are creating our pain, which is why it is important to challenge them. Just like we can begin mastering our feelings, we can master our thoughts. In fact, if we start changing our thoughts, by reframing them in a positive way, positive feelings will follow.

As you become more conscious of your thoughts, when situations arise, you can now look at them to see if you have accurately assessed them. You are usually looking at your present through glasses that have been colored by the past. This is one of the basic premises of cognitive behavior theories. According to cognitive behavioral therapists, all distress is a result of a person's response to a situation. It is important to understand that situations are neither good nor bad; rather, our perceptions label the situations one way or another. We don't see things as they are, but instead appraise them using irrational beliefs.

Believe it or not, we actually have a choice whether or not a situation will cause us to feel distress. We don't usually think in this way, because our emotional responses are generally automatic. When something happens, we do have a moment to stop, pause, and assess the situation. By practicing the methods illustrated in this book, you will be more aware of this process, and hopefully be able to slow down the emotional process.

The next time you are faced with a situation that causes you to feel stressed--whether it involve anger, sadness, anxiety, etc.--it is important to stop and identify the thought that preceded the emotion. The term stress is used often throughout this book to describe any negative response. Then you want to ask yourself some questions. One question might be, "What feeling is this situation triggering? Why?" Other questions include: "How could I have seen the situation differently," "Am I exaggerating or over-generalizing," or "What facts are not consistent with my thinking?" Because our emotions sometimes tend to get out of control, you can also ask yourself, "Am I going to allow this external situation to have power over me? Is this situation really worth getting stressed over?" Usually the answer is no, because we know some of the detrimental effects of stress. As we all know, it causes us physical harm and is a major contributor to illnesses. When we are stressed, this prevents us from effectively solving problems and more importantly, finding inner peace. Once you start seeing the origins of stress-provoking thoughts, you can start to realize that they are no longer accurate, or productive.

Jane became very upset and sad when her boss pointed out a mistake she had made. But then she thought to herself, why am I upset? She realized that she thought that he is always picking on her. He is always criticizing her and no one else, which made her feel she was a failure. She became very anxious, wondering if she would be fired for this mistake. After examining the situation, however, she realized that her boss was not picking on her. It is his job to point out mistakes, and she is probably not the only one being criticized. She also realized that it was irrational for her to feel like a failure and be anxious about possibly losing her job. She was exaggerating the situation.

Again, it is also important to not only challenge these beliefs, but identify their origins as well. Jane realized that when she is criticized, she tends to over-react, because these criticisms trigger scars from her past. Jane decided that she was no longer going to allow the pain from her past to continue upsetting her in the present. She realized she did not need to feel hurt when her boss made a critical comment.

The goal of these exercises is to become consciously more aware of your thought process and emotional life. It is only when you start living more consciously can you truly feel empowered. It is important to make space for this process in your life and decide that this is something you will master. You can make the decision to no longer be the victim of your thoughts and feelings, but this process can only occur by continuing to look inward.

Reflection

Most of us live our lives without ever understanding our thoughts and emotions. These thoughts and feelings prevent us from finding inner peace. Experiences we encounter during our childhood create emotional scars. Our present circumstances trigger feelings that erupt from these scars. We carry all of these emotional scars and dysfunctional thinking into our present, until they are made conscious, addressed, and processed. They impact every moment of our lives and motivate our decisions. Therefore, the first step of discovering inner peace is to heal from our past, which means examining and understanding the past and how it impacts us presently. Have you identified the thoughts and feelings that prevent you from finding inner peace? Have you identified where these thoughts and feelings originated?

Healing from our past consists of several steps, including: self-reflection, validating your emotions, feeling your feelings, and challenging your beliefs and perceptions. This assists us in gaining mastery over our thoughts and feelings in the present.

Have you taken the time to reflect?

Have you validated your feelings and truly felt them?

Have you challenged your thoughts and beliefs?

This part of your journey is a step by step process. So, as you reflect upon the situations that currently cause you feelings of distress, here is a protocol you can use:

1. When you feel distressed: Pause. Take a deep breathe. Sit still.
2. Become very clear of your thoughts and your feelings.
3. Validate these feelings.
4. Feel them fully without acting on them.
5. Try to determine where these thoughts and feelings come from.
6. Can you challenge the thoughts and beliefs you have about this situation?
7. What is the negative result of your distress? Is this something that is not serving you in a positive way?
8. Can you let it go?

9. If not, why not? Continue exploring why you are holding on to this feeling?

10. If yes, what did you learn about yourself through this experience? Feel the release of the negative energy.

PHILOSOPHICAL PRINCIPLES

The goal of healing from the past is to gain mastery over your emotions and thoughts, since it is these unexplored and unresolved feelings that keep us from finding peace within our lives. Through the process of discovering inner peace, you will start to notice that you are taking control over your life. This new found peace is your way to freedom, because you will no longer be a victim to your thoughts, feelings, and external factors. As you continue becoming empowered, your philosophy of life, so to speak, becomes your guide through this process, which is why it is important to incorporate sound philosophies that guide your everyday living.

This process will allow you to live with more conscious awareness of your thoughts and feelings, which will enable you to be the author of your life. This is important to the process of inner peace, because you will now be in charge of present, not unresolved past emotions. Committing to a life guided by philosophical principles assists you in living consciously and with intention. To further strengthen your mastery over your emotions and thoughts, there are philosophical principles that are also important to incorporate into your daily life. These principles will help you remain at peace as you deal with new situations. These principles represent wisdom discovered through the ages that can remedy our suffering, which can then lead to inner peace. When you encounter a negative feeling, it is helpful to examine some of these philosophical teachings as a way of coping.

Conscious and intentional living is something that you need to practice and reinforce every day, as it is not how we usually live our lives. All too often, we allow external sources, such as work and family obligations, to dictate our day. However, with this new approach to life, it is important to set aside time each day in order to start the process of intentionally creating the life you want.

There are many ways to put this into practice. One way is to start each day with intention, because all too often we allow external factors to dictate our lives, and we find ourselves living on autopilot. This is why it is important to slow down, take control, and not allow these external factors to dictate our behavior. This is the key to living intentionally, not reactively. So, each day, it is important to start the day centered and in control.

It may also be helpful to have visual reminders, such as meaningful sayings or referencing books. Or you can set aside time each day to reflect or journal. Maybe each morning, you read an inspirational quote or a meaningful passage as a way to start your day. You might also choose to schedule practices such as yoga and meditation to help you take the time to reflect and slow down. At the beginning of the week, you might start the day by reflecting on the previous week, and begin fresh, with good intentions.

Here are some principles that you might choose to adopt as part of your personal philosophy of life. They include: accepting that we can only control ourselves; letting go of expectations; looking internally for happiness and self-validation; accepting the present and the past; and forgiving and understanding others.

We Can Only Control Ourselves

Each one has to find his peace from within. And peace to be real must be unaffected by outside circumstances

–Ghandi

Many of us struggle with finding inner peace, because we desire to control external factors, such as other people and the condition around us. Although we have all heard the serenity prayer "Grant me the serenity to accept the things that I cannot change, change the things I can, and the wisdom to know the difference," do we really know what this means, and are we putting it into practice? Let's examine the serenity prayer. "Grant me the serenity to accept the things I cannot change." This means the world around us; in fact, it is possibly everything but ourselves. "Change the things I can." This takes into consideration how I look at things and react to the external world. "And the wisdom to know the difference." This calls us to continually understand that we have little or no control over anything except ourselves. Often, we are upset, angry, sad, frustrated, etc. due to our desire to have control over situations. If we learn to relinquish control over external factors, we can attain a sense of peace.

This idea is very different from what most of us were raised to think, and the messages we received from the world around us. We spend most of our physical and emotional energy trying to have an impact on our universe, while never really having control over ourselves.

Why is it, actually, that we feel the need to control our external environment? There are two main reasons why we seek to control our external environment. The first is fear, primarily about the future. The second is being attached to a desired outcome, which will be discussed in the next section.

Let's take a common situation. Jane fears that her boyfriend may betray her. The idea that she cannot watch over him all the time causes her to feel anxiety. She sometimes finds herself playing detective and looking for clues to make sure he is not cheating on her. She can learn to understand that this anxiety is caused because she fears that he will leave, and she has attached a lot of meaning to this. If he cheats or leaves, this may mean to her that she is not good enough in some way. She can only find peace by understanding that she cannot control him, and that this is okay. She finally arrives at the understanding that whether he cheats or not, in reality, is not a reflection on her; his cheating or leaving is a result of his emotional baggage, so to speak.

She can find peace in understanding that she can learn to live with whatever the outcome will be, as long as she can detach herself from it.

An important question to ask is, do we have control over our environment and, if so, to what extent? There are conflicting views regarding this issue. The law of attraction, which is based on quantum theory, suggests that we are able to influence our environment. The observer with conscious intent can effectuate action. This contradicts the Eastern approach such as Buddhism, which suggests that we have little or no control over external events.

There is another idea, which bridges both seemingly opposing views. First, we need to understand that we are energy and are integrated in an energy field, our universe. We have an effect on the energy field—the world—and it has an effect on us. And there are many factors impacting our energy field, such as our unconscious beliefs, other people's energy, and possibly millions of other things.

A different way of looking at it is that there is no such thing as control, per se. How can we possibly control external factors if in fact we are a part of the universe? If we were to control something, this would imply that we are separate from it, which is not the case. Therefore, we need to focus on living in harmony with our world, because we are part of a bigger whole, not independent of it.

It is important to deal with things as they come without any negative emotions attached. Once we have attached negative emotions, inner peace is lost. Although we have an impact on the world around us, at the present moment, it is important is to accept our present as it is because our present is just as it is supposed to be. The only thing that we can control in the present is ourselves, and how we react to situations and what actions we choose to take.

For example, Jane was very stressed about her financial situation. She had incurred some debt, and whenever she gets her credit card bill, she would become very upset and think, "I don't know if I can ever get out of this situation. I feel hopeless. I am such a failure because I cannot manage my money." This would leave her feeling sad for days and she would have a difficult time sleeping, because she was worrying about this situation. Jane cannot change her current reality, her credit card debt. However, her sadness and insomnia are not helping the situation. Furthermore, her appraisal of herself and her feelings of hopelessness may be preventing her from finding a solution. The only thing she can do is develop a way to reduce her debt. She can do this by getting a part-time job, eliminating some expense or restructuring her finances. Although she can apply for these positions, ultimately, the decision is out of her control.

Again, she can find peace in accepting her present, which means that she is fully okay with her present situation, doing what she can in the moment and learning to live with the outcome.

Letting Go of Expectations and Desires, which Leads to Acceptance of the Present and the Past

When I let go of what I am, I become what I might be.
- *Lao Tzu*

In addition to accepting that we may have little or no control over external factors and circumstances, we need to let go of our expectations and desires. It is important that we live our lives not being attached to the outcome of situations, which will bring us peace.

One of the main premises of Buddhism is that our suffering is created by our desires and expectations. Think about your current situation. List all the reasons that you are unhappy or not feeling at peace. When you examine this list, most, if not all of the items on the list involve desires or expectations.

For example, you may feel worried because you have too many bills. This worry stems from your expectation that you should have financial security. Or, if you are unhappy because you don't like your job, it is your desire to have a better job. If we just accepted our situation the way it is without judgment, we could eliminate our suffering. This does not mean that we should not try to eliminate our debt or find a better job, but it means that we can find peace within our present circumstances and make changes without emotional attachment.

If we come from a place of peace, we will ultimately make the best choices and feel empowered by these choices. This means not feeling anxious about our debt, frustrated about the job or fearful about our future, but accepting what is in the present moment.

We have expectations of how things "should be." We have a picture of how our life should be, how our family should be, how others should treat us, how much money we should be making, what job we should have, etc. These expectations are what create our suffering because, frequently, our present does not resemble what we think it should. We become victims of the images we create and the thoughts that we have about how things should be, which creates un-peacefulness.

This picture that we create about how the world should look comes from many sources. As mentioned earlier, during our formative years, we fantasize about the world and ourselves to cope with our suffering. We also receive messages from our families and society about what is

39

acceptable. All of these expectations lead us to pain because sometimes our life is not what we think is ideal and, as we learned earlier, we do not have control over external sources. These desires and expectations also keep us from living in the now, so we are unable to find peace and happiness in our present. As discussed earlier, and will be explored in detail later, it is our ego that judges our reality and creates our expectations, which generates our suffering.

Jane is feeling very distressed that she is single. She feels that at her age, she should be married and starting a family. In order for her to find peace in her life, it is important for her to accept her situation. It is her expectation that she should be married that is creating her unhappiness. At the present moment, she is single, which she can look at as a fact, not a judgment. She attaches meaning to her reality that she is single.

Some of the meaning she attaches to this is that she is inferior if she is not married and fears that her time is running out. Who says that she can't be happy being single? Does this really matter? If so, by whose rules does it matter? She may want to explore why this is so important for her.

Nonetheless, by accepting this, she could find peace in her present. Furthermore, she thinks that if she is single now, she may never get married. Just because she is single now has nothing to do with her future. If she approaches the dating scene with anxiety and hopelessness, she will not have a positive experience.

Think about all the items on your list that are creating unhappiness. How can you start accepting each one without judgment? For example, if you have many bills, instead of letting this situation creating a feeling of anxiety, you can reframe it by thinking, "My bills are where they are, and I am in the process of finding a solution." If you are finding this task difficult—maybe there is one item on your list that you feel you cannot accept—you need to explore why it is so important. You are probably attaching some meaning to it, making further exploration necessary.

If you really feel that there is no way you can make peace with your financial situation, ask yourself, "Why is this so important to me?" You may find that you feel your financial situation means something to you. Is it that you feel your self-worth is based on this or is it the fear that you will not have money? It is important to get to the root of these factors to start eliminating our desires and expectations. Remember, you created these desires and expectations, so you can eliminate them. You are in control.

Inner peace is achieved when we lose our attachment to our desires and can see the reality in our current situation without judgment. You can find peace and appreciate what is instead of lamenting what is not. Letting go of expectations and desires can be quite profound, leading you to feel at peace with your present. It is important to keep in mind that you and your life are exactly how they are supposed to be at the present time. This may be a difficult idea to grasp during a time of adversity, however, it is important to keep in mind that there is a reason the universe has created the situation you are in right now. And instead of judging it, realize that at some time you will understand the lesson that is to be learned.

A thought to keep in mind, and something of which I continually remind myself, is, "My life is (or I am) perfect, with all of its (my) imperfections. I have exactly everything I need right now. My life is exactly how it needs to be at the present." Once we let go of our expectations and desires, we can accept our present and past. Inner peace is found when one accepts his or her life as it is in that particular moment, and not in desiring it to be anything different from what it is. Even during the most trying times, it is important to accept the present for what and how it is without judgment. It is also important to remember that the universe never gives you something you cannot handle. This too shall pass. We often judge how our present should be, but we really miss out on appreciating the moment. Even in the most trying times, it is important to embrace the present exactly how it is and trust that what we are going through in the moment is important for personal growth.

In addition to accepting our present, it is equally important to accept our past, no matter how terrible it is. Many of us curse the past, hate the things that have happened, detest those who have wronged us, and question why these things happened to us. No matter how terrible the trauma, it is important that we accept it, because in reality, there is nothing we can do about our past, and being upset about it does not change things. Realistically, the past does not exist. It is only a figment of our minds. Judging the past only creates pain for you in the present. How is your past impacting your present moment? Is it keeping you from feeling at peace? If so, it may be important to continue healing from the past until all the work is done. Instead of judging the past, it is important to find meaning in what has happened.

There are many reasons why we have not accepted the past. If we have not healed from the past, it is difficult to accept it and let it go. Many times, we hold on to the hurt and anger of our past because we want to punish those who have wronged us. But being angry only punishes us in the present. We also hold on to the anger, anxiety, fear, etc. of the past because we think this will protect us in the present.

We have to keep in mind that the past as nothing to do with our present or future unless we allow it. For example, just because you have been hurt in the past does not mean that you will be hurt in the present or in the future. If we understand that others cannot hurt us, there really is no reason to need protection. We have to understand that the past cannot be changed; all that can be changed is how we feel about it in the present, and by not accepting it is only negatively impacting us in the present.

Jane feels that she has been wronged in the past, so she clings to this anger as a way of protecting herself from getting hurt. However, being angry does not necessarily facilitate this goal and only hurts her and prevents her from developing healthy relationships with others. We can learn to embrace our past, no matter how terrible. Without those experiences, we would not be who we are. It is in the face of adversity that we grow. Very little growth is achieved when things are going well for us. The idea is to trust that the universe is providing you with all that you need at the moment and be thankful for these experiences of personal growth. Without trauma, conflict, and obstacles we would have no opportunities for growth.

This is often difficult to grasp during times of adversity, because we are usually impacted by our emotions in such cases. We can, though, view adversity in a different way, for instance as an opportunity to learn about our selves.

At some point during our process of self-growth, it is important to forgive those that have hurt us in the past. Many find it hard to forgive others for hurting them; we want to punish those who wronged us. Holding on to this anger only punishes you. Forgiving is really a gift that we give ourselves. By holding on to anger, resentment, and hurt feelings, you only hurt your self. To feel at peace, it is important to forgive others. You can still believe that what they did was wrong, and you can forgive without agreeing with them. Many feel that if they forgive, it is a way of condoning past actions. Letting go of the anger is not condoning what has happened. Often, we confuse forgiveness with forgetting. When you forgive, you don't forget what has happened, but the negative emotions no longer follow the thought. Remember: forgiveness is not an emotion, but a choice. A choice that is important in finding peace.

We also have difficulty forgiving, because we still desire that person to right the wrong they committed. But, as mentioned earlier, those expectations cause us pain. We cannot right the wrong that has happened. Once you have let go of the pain, the process of forgiveness becomes easier. What feelings are you still holding on to? Who have you not forgiven? Why is it difficult for you to forgive?

Sometimes, we can seek forgiveness once we understand why others did what they did. For example, we have to remember that our parents are people with pasts and they did the best they could with the tools that they had. Others hurt us because they have not dealt with their own emotional demons. If you find that you are not ready to forgive, you may want to ask yourself why not, what is this feeling serving? We frequently think that if we do not forgive, we are in a way still punishing the person. But in actually we are only punishing ourselves.

In addition to forgiving others, we should also seek to understand and be patient with them. Just as our unresolved emotional scars dictate our behavior, others experience the same dynamic. It is not uncommon that, once you understand your dynamic, you want others to be the same way. However, it is important to understand that others are not necessarily on the same path as you. It is impossible to change someone who is not seeking change.

It is important not to have expectations and think that we can change others. All that we can do is be an example and share with others who are interested in sharing. This is something difficult because some of us feel, "Why should I be so tolerant?" Remember, though, that your expectations are only hurting you. Anytime you judge or have expectations of others, such as when thinking someone is a "bad" person, this creates negative energy that is only hurting you. It is best to always seek to understand others. Something I keep in mind is the belief that there are no bad people, but only people who are behaving badly due to their emotional circumstances, such as hurt and fear. When you come from a place of understanding, not judging, this is a place of peace.

Ask yourself, "Why am I not happy at this moment?" The answer will probably be "Because I have not accepted my current reality," or "I am angry about the past." Can you, right now, accept your current reality? If the answer is, "No, I want something different," you must remember that it is your expectations about the present and the past that will keep you from being truly happy and at peace. If you are struggling with this, you may need to go back to the first section to discover how to overcome this obstacle.

Living in the Moment

The secret of health for both mind and body is not to mourn for the past, worry about the future, or anticipate troubles, but to live in the present moment wisely and earnestly.

-Buddha

In addition to wanting control over external things, having desires, and not accepting our past and present, we are not at peace because we are not in the present moment. We are either lamenting over the past, worrying about the future or judging our present. Think about the moment that you are in at this minute. You are reading this book. The moment is (hopefully) peaceful. When is this peacefulness interrupted? It is when you break away from the moment and start thinking about the list of things you should be doing instead of reading? This is judging the present. Or is it when you start wondering about what needs to be done later. This is living in the future. Once you leave the moment, you are no longer feeling peaceful. When you start living in the future, you are no longer in the moment. When you are judging the moment, you are not living in the moment, because this judgment is created by past appraisals.

Living in the future causes anxiety. Hurt, sadness, guilt, and resentment occur when we live in the past. Here is the irony. Both past and future do not exist. The only thing that truly exists is the moment that you are in right now. Yesterday only exists in our thoughts; therefore, it is not real. The future certainly does not exist. If we really think about it, how healthy is it to be preoccupied by something that does not exist--the past and the future? How much time do you spend living in the past or future?

Think about your last vacation. Why do you think vacations are such pleasurable activities? It is primarily because you were in the moment. For example, if you traveled to an exotic destination, you were immersed in this newness. The unfamiliar sights kept you focused on the moment. Day-to-day, however, most of us experience something that shifts our attention away from the moment, such as a delayed flight or lost hotel reservation. But you can remain in that moment without judgment. You can accept that it is your reality that your flight was delayed or you lost your hotel reservation. You don't need to go on vacation to practice living in the moment. Any activity that you are doing, even working or performing a mundane task such as doing the dishes, can be done in the moment by focusing and staying present, and not letting the mind wander by thinking ahead or judging the moment.

Ultimate peace is when you can be in the midst of a terrible situation and just let go of all negativity. Jane had this experience. She was facing extreme adversity. She decided to take a long walk along the lake. For a moment, she stopped thinking about her situation and really looked at the scenery. She realized how truly beautiful and blue the water was and saw the magnificence of the clouds. The moment was beautiful. She thought to herself: Who was she to judge or disturb it? That is when she decided to just let her negative emotions go. The things in her life were just insignificant details she realized, and she saw a bigger picture that enabled her to find a sense of peace in her present reality. She didn't judge it. She just accepted it for what it was.

The moment is precious because that is all we really have. The past and the future never truly exist. Ask yourself, are you frequently rushing through life, only focusing on the future? Are you frequently judging the present moment in a critical way? Are you frequently upset about the past? It is important to cherish every moment, because there is never any certainty that there will be another. You are probably thinking: Well, what do I do if the moment is terrible? It is important to keep in mind that it is you who are labeling it terrible. It is more appropriate to acknowledge the situation for what it is, accept it without judging, and decide what you can do right now to deal with the situation at hand. Judging your reality is only keeping you from finding peace within the moment.

Living in the moment is something that needs to be practiced with intention. You can start practicing it at any moment just by making the decision to be in the moment. You can choose to set aside a block of time to fully be in the moment—at work, relaxing at home, or on vacation—and then practice being in the moment by focusing on what you are doing. So, even if you are sitting and sipping a cup of tea, do not shift to mental auto-pilot, allowing your mind to race to the past or future, but rather focus on the task at hand. Be in your body, be in the experience. If you are taking a walk, focus on what is around you, feel your body, feel the experience. If you notice your thoughts drifting to something other than the present, just continue refocusing your attention on it. As you practice, it becomes easier. When a negative feeling arises, this is a sign that you are not in the moment, and all you need to do is to get centered and start again.

We are in Control of our Pain

Nobody can hurt me without my permission.

–Ghandi

Why is it that we believe others or external circumstances can hurt us? It is important to keep in mind that it is the thoughts we have regarding others that trigger emotions in us. It is our emotion that hurts us, not necessarily other people or external circumstances. What happens is, the dynamic that occurs in a relationship or how perceived situations trigger an emotional scar, which is why we take what others do to us so personally. It is important to take ownership over our thoughts and feelings. Often times, these emotions, such as hurt, appear to happen so automatically, we do not realize that we have that second to make a choice and decide not to be hurt. Until now, no one taught us that we had a choice. However, once we have awareness of our thoughts and feelings, it is important to remember that no one can make us feel something that we do not choose to feel.

This happens with conscious living. With it, we learn to stop and pause before the emotion occurs. If we feel hurt by someone, this hurt is not truly what is happening now, but it is merely the trigger for the hurt that has always been there. When we feel hurt by someone else, or by something that happened, we need to look inward to understand why that creates pain for us.

Jane's partner has been working a lot, and she is starting to feel hurt because she thinks, "If he loved me, he would want to spend more time with me." In her mind, her being special has to do with how much attention she receives from her partner. She wonders if she is special and she feels hurt because she believes that his action indicates that she is not. He is not causing her to feel hurt: rather, she misperceives that because he is working a lot, she is not special. Her pain of not feeling special has nothing to do with her current situation. Instead, it is triggering feelings from her own childhood, when she felt that her father worked too much and she believed that, if she were special, he would change. She did not understand that her father working as much as he did had nothing to do with her. She is special no matter what. Once she gains an understanding of this, she can decide not to take her partner's actions so personally.

In relationships we often use past paradigms, thinking that we can predict what will happen in relationships. If we have been betrayed in the past, we will convince ourselves that the person we are presently in a relationship with will betray us. Because we are so afraid of the pain, we can often avoid or even sabotage relationships. We sometimes do not take advantage of present opportunities, because we are clouded by our predetermined thoughts and judgments. By doing this, we prevent ourselves from truly enjoying the relationship and getting close. If we enter into a relationship, we can also misconstrue others' actions and words to justify our beliefs.

Self-Validation

To thine own self be true.

-Shakespeare

Our pursuit of validation from others and outside sources also creates suffering. We frequently look for others to validate us or define who we are, or we look for external things such as status, money, or power to define who we are. As with our expectation that external things can provide us with happiness, wanting validation from external sources gives power to external factors, ones usually beyond our control.

An important principle to keep in mind is that only you can validate your existence. If you are defining yourself by something external, you will be the victim of this external source. You are giving away your power. List all of the things that you believe validate your existence: your title, your degrees, your friends, your significant other, your family, your paycheck, etc. If you were to throw that list away and no longer had that degree, job, or loved one, would that change who you are? It should not. And if it feels as if it would, this puts you in a powerless place. It is important to understand that these external things can change. Are you giving up your power to external factors? This may be why you are stuck in a certain situation. For example, you may want to give up that high-paying job to pursue your life passion, but are afraid because the title or the paycheck is defining you.

An inherent problem in relationships is that most of us seek validation from our partners. For example, we want someone else to validate that we are special, possibly because we did not feel as though we received this validation from our parents. We believe that only when someone loves us, we are special. However, this gives a lot of power to others. Also, we frequently need continuous reinforcement that our partner might not be able to provide us. What happens when you are not in a relationship--does this mean you are not special? How much proof does the other person need to provide you to show you that you are special?

Jane recently met someone new and, despite the fact that everything went well on the first date, he never called her again. She thought, as a result, that she is not good enough, and felt rejected and hurt. This feeling of hurt is not just because of current perceived rejection, but because it opened wounds from the past. There are many reasons why the person might not have called. But she interpreted the situation based on the idea that she is only special if someone wants to be with her.

Her experience can be an opportunity for personal growth, by pushing her to examine her feelings and to work on changing them. She may ask herself, Why do I feel hurt? What is it about me and about my past that I need to understand better? She can change her appraisal of the situation, such as by thinking, "I am a wonderful person and obviously this other person was not ready to be in a relationship," or "Other people don't validate my self-worth." It is important to ask yourself, Is this because I don't feel special due to something in my past, and am looking for my partner to validate me? It may be, and usually is, that other peoples' actions have nothing to do with you, yet you perceive that they do. "If something happens, it's because of me." This idea comes about because, as children, we truly believed the world revolved around us.

Everything that did or did not happen was personal and we still bring some of those ideas into our current life. If someone breaks up with us, for example, sometimes we wonder "Why did they do that to me?" We question our sense of self. What did I do wrong? Am I not good enough? It is important to remember that we all have our own agendas and we make decisions based on what we feel is best for us. It may not even be the best decision, depending on our motivation. Remember, the decisions that others make generally have nothing to do with us.

Understanding Existential Concerns

Believe nothing, no matter where you read it, or who said it, no matter if I have said it, unless it agrees with your own reason and your own common sense.

–Buddha

It is important to add existential concerns to our repertoire of philosophical principles. Some of these existential concerns include being authentic, finding meaning in our lives and our suffering, living in a life-affirming way, accepting aloneness, and becoming the author of our lives. According to existential philosophy and psychology, the existential aim in life is the individual's search for meaning and purpose through the discovery of one's authentic self. The process by which we discover our purpose and authentic self leads us to a feeling of peacefulness.

There are some existential concerns that we all face as part of our human experience. Our life path creates feelings of anxiety, stress, sadness, frustration, hatred, disappointment, frustration, and many other unsettling feelings. We also suffer because we seek to find meaning in a seemingly meaningless universe. These feelings lead us to some fundamental obstacles in achieving inner peace. There are obstacles such as being involved in the human drama and being inauthentic, which distract us from our existential journey. Furthermore, our past, if not addressed, keeps us stuck in the human drama, with ourselves and with others, and we are unable to move further along our path of personal growth and discovery of inner peace.

The human drama is something that we experience every day. It is the drama that is played out with others and ourselves when we have not resolved our emotional scars. The human drama can take many forms. It is the hurt we feel when others have rejected, angered, or disappointed us. It is the need for love and approval from others. It is the conflicts that we encounter with others and within ourselves. All of these negative human emotions distract us from understanding what life is truly about. It is when we free ourselves of this human drama that we can achieve a sense of peace. When we can live without feeling hurt, frustrated, disappointed, or angry, we can live in peace. Once we achieve this, we can live authentically and in a life-affirming way. Once we have healed from our scars, we can find personal meaning because our pain no longer distracts us. Once we have healed from our scars, we are no longer the victim, and we can become the author of our lives.

Being Authentic and Becoming the Author of Your Life

Being authentic is knowing ourselves and being ourselves as we engage with others in the activity of leadership - no playing roles, no acting, no fulfilling the expectations of others. We are actually and exactly who we are. Nothing false, nothing imitative, nothing imaginary.

-Moxley

Being authentic is living as who we are, not by the roles that we have designed for ourselves or that others have created for us. We are all born authentic, but spend a significant amount of time wearing masks, whereby we learn to act a certain way in given situations. We learn to wear these masks because, as we grow, in order to survive, we want to please those around us. But we do not know how, so we learn social rules. When we go out into the world, instead of being ourselves, we desire approval, acceptance, and love from others and feel we need to wear masks to get that approval. We play a role, because we are afraid or ashamed to be our true selves. These roles are taken from images we develop of how we should be, after we are exposed to parents, friends, peers, the media, etc. Being authentic is taking off the masks that you wear and being the person who you truly are.

When we begin to live true to ourselves, we accept who we are and begin to be authentic, not only with ourselves but also with others. We learn to have real relationships with others, because we have explored and processed all the reasons we want to manipulate others. When we do this, we learn to truly love and care for others, no longer using others to satisfy our psychological needs. When we are authentic, we take charge of our lives and learn that we have the freedom to create our own existence. Being authentic is also being honest about your thoughts and feelings and about when your behavior matches with your values.

The key to living authentically is filtering out those other voices and finding your authentic voice. At any given moment, it seems there are at least three voices in your head: your authentic voice, the voice of your family, and a societal voice. All of these voices, bouncing off one another, can create inner conflict, so it is important to find your authentic voice and cast off the others.

Is there something you truly would like to do, but are conflicted about due to fears that are presenting themselves? For example, are you unhappy with your current career choice, and have you always dreamt of something else, but wondered about its feasibility or practicality? It is important to determine whose voices are spreading this doubt. If your authentic self truly wants to pursue something different, you need to challenge the voices of your family and society, which may have created a sense of fear in you.

Jane wants to be an artist. She believes that she is creative and has many talents. Often she fantasizes about leaving her mundane nine-to-five job to pursue her true passion. There are times when she has attempted to pursue a career in a more creative field, but is stopped by her thoughts. She wonders if this is practical and if she is good enough. This creates feelings of fear. However, she can challenge these thoughts. She can ask herself, why is being practical important. Is it important to her or is it really only important to her family? Besides, many people make a living in creative careers. Furthermore, she knows she has talents. It is the voice of others that questions this. By filtering out these voices, she can follow her authentic passion.

The following is another exercise you can use. Identify an unhappy situation in your life. Ask yourself, "Why am I in this situation," "How is this situation compromising my authentic self," "What is the fear that is driving my decision," or "Whose voice am I listening to?"

If you are unhappy with your job, ask yourself, "Why do I continue to stay and be unfulfilled at my job, day after day?" Ask yourself, "Does this profession represent who I am authentically?"

If you truly want to do something different, ask yourself, "What am I afraid of?" Often, it is the voice of our family or society telling us that these choices may not be feasible. There will always be an inner conflict, if we act to please others or do what is expected, instead of following that authentic voice. Therefore, one of the steps to inner peace is filtering out those other voices in our head, and allowing the authentic self to emerge.

Once you choose to follow your authentic voice, you may also feel some tension. This is perfectly normal, because frequently it is fear that has dictated your behavior. It takes courage to be authentic, and your choices truly determine the person you want to become. You have the freedom to create your own life. To be authentic means to define your own definition of success, not what society or others deem as successful. To live authentically, you must be free from these cultural restraints and think for yourself to create a life that is authentically yours.

Do you ever wonder why it is important that you live a certain way, have the job that you have, or own a certain car or house? We are often working in jobs that we hate, because of our title or the paycheck. Is it worth sacrificing your happiness or health? Sometimes, we are even working at jobs that are not aligned with our personal beliefs, but try to look the other way because we think that it is worth sacrificing our beliefs for the paycheck. However, are you able to sleep well at night?

Jane works as a pharmaceutical representative and is not happy with her job for many reasons. One reason is that she personally does not believe in pharmaceuticals as they are promoted in our society. She is aware of how potentially unsafe they can be and sees other safer alternatives to illnesses. However, she enjoys the benefits of the job such as the pay, but is finding it difficult to continue working in this capacity due to her personal beliefs. And this prevents her from sleeping well at night. She can learn to challenge the thoughts that prevent her from finding a career that is more in line with her personal beliefs, which will bring her a sense of peace.

This is the true test of your authenticity. Start to practice conscious living, by understanding why you make the decisions you make. You are responsible for your actions, but also for your failure to act. This discovery can be anxiety provoking, because it is the awakening of the realization that you have the responsibility to take control over your life and your destiny. But once you start practicing authenticity, this anxiety will diminish.

Finding Meaning

He who has a why can endure any how.

-Nietzche

Feelings that can keep us from finding peace include emptiness and restlessness. Many of us question what life is really about. By resolving human drama and becoming authentic, we can find meaning in our lives. We can also find meaning in our suffering, which can help us accept our past and our present suffering.

As we learned earlier, only we can validate our existence and we must not give the power to others to do so. This means we create our own idea of personal success and meaning in our lives, and not base them on what society deems successful. We can free ourselves from cultural expectations and create our own life, full of personal meaning.

By finding personal meaning in our lives, we trust in the purpose and direction of our journey. By living with our beliefs, we know the direction that we are meant to go, and we trust the universe will lead the way. But it is only when our mind, body, and soul are at peace that we can truly fulfill our destiny. By resolving the human drama, we do not consume ourselves with negative emotions and distract ourselves from our journey. By being authentic, we eliminate the anxiety about who we are supposed to be; we begin to live our own lives.

When we find meaning and purpose, all the anxiety and hopelessness and fear disappear. Our mission guides us. We become aware that we have authorship of our lives and start to take responsibility over our destiny, feelings, and even our suffering. We then create our own life meaning, by creating our unique purpose in life. So, the question is, "What is life's unique purpose? What is meaningful to you? What is the meaning of your suffering?"

Living in a Life-Affirming Way

It is possible to 'say yes to life' in spite of all the tragic aspects of human existence.

-Viktor Frankl

A question to ask your self is "Am I truly living and making decisions that are life-affirming, or I am making choices based on fear?" Think about the decisions that you make: are they truly positive and life-affirming, or are they created out of fear—fear of being hurt, fear of death, fear of pain, fear of the unknown, etc. When you start to think about the choices you make, you will find that you make many decisions out of fear, which keeps you from living fully. Living in a life-affirming way is the difference between thriving and merely surviving.

The greatest fear that is not widely discussed is the fear of death. In order to go forward in one's personal growth, it is essential to embrace the idea that we are all going to die. This is the only thing in life that we are certain of, and we don't know exactly when it will happen nor can we avoid it from happening despite all of our best efforts. Most of us do not want to think about death, but by confronting death, we can live a full, authentic, happy life.

To live life fully, it is important to accept that it ends. It is sometimes in the face of death that you begin to truly live. Stephen Levine once said, "Most of us go to extraordinary lengths to ignore, laugh off, or deny the fact that we are going to die, but preparing for death is one of the most rational and rewarding acts of a lifetime." A real confrontation with death usually causes one to question what is meaningful and important. Have you ever heard someone that has been diagnosed with a life-threatening illness say, "I wish I had spent more time working." Almost everybody says, "I wish I'd spent time doing the things I wanted to do--traveling, spending time with others, being closer with my family, having fun, etc."

Many individuals have experienced life-altering changes after being confronted with their mortality, such as having someone close to them die or having been diagnosed with a terminal illness. As existentialist psychotherapist Irvin Yalom said, "Although the physicality of death destroys man, the idea of death saves him."

If you knew that you only had a short time to live, how would you live your life? How is that different from how you are living it today? As you start to explore these questions, you will come to learn that many of the decisions we make are based on fear, conscious or unconscious, such as fear of death, pain, rejection, and lack of control.

One of the reasons that we fear death is that we fear the unknown and the idea of not being. Death is in the future and our preoccupation with it keeps us from living. However, the idea that we die can spark us to appreciate every moment we have, primarily by causing us to make choices not based on fear, but based on thriving and living in a life-affirming way.

This idea is also helpful in understanding how important it is to live in the moment. In our relationships, we are afraid of rejection, getting hurt, and abandonment, and this prevents us from taking emotional risks. These wounds, as we discussed earlier, sometimes motivate us to make choices based on self-protection or survival. Keep in mind what you learned above: that you own your feelings and no one can make you feel a certain way. Your wounds cloud your reality, and you make choices that do not allow you to thrive. It is beautiful to love as if you have never been hurt, because loving fully is living fully in the now, not in the past or future.

Our fears keep us from living authentically. So instead of working at a job that you hate because you need security, while wondering if you can make it as a . . . you fill in the blank, pick a career that brings you contentment, joy, and something that you look forward to after waking up in the morning. What are the things that you are doing out of fear? What changes can you make to live in a more life-affirming way?

Accepting Aloneness

No one saves us but ourselves. No one can and no one may. We ourselves must walk the path.

-Buddha

Existential theorists claim that one of the basic existential concerns that we have is to desire connection with others. The feeling of loneliness is a malady we all face. Theorists surmise that this may be due to the fear of dying alone. It is also that the ego, which will be discussed in detail later, feels separate from others and yearns for connectedness. It is important to embrace this loneliness and realize that, in fact, we are alone in the sense that we come into the world alone, we must go on our life journey alone, and we die alone. Overcoming this aloneness is conquering the fear of being alone and understanding that no matter how close we are to another person, there is a distance between us and that distance is okay.

Sometimes we also fear being alone because we have not figured out how to resolve our emotional pain. And we discover that others can be there to soothe us, making us crave them. As discussed earlier, we can find ways to cope with our own feelings, which can create a sense of power.

In my years of dealing with clients, I have discovered something quite interesting. One of the most common crises that most people encounter is the feeling of loneliness and not fitting in. I don't think that I have ever encountered one person who ever felt like they belonged. If most people don't belong, who actually does belong, and what are we all trying so hard to belong to. I feel that this spiritual yearning of connectedness comes from past experiences of being misunderstood and unloved or unwanted. We all want to be connected to a group, but there are fears of being rejected, abandoned, unloved, and abused. But we all belong, because we each share the same thing. We are all wounded, and I wonder if this is the reason why we are here. We are all wounded by our pasts and, although we may have different wounds, we all are searching for similar things. This is what truly connects us. We are all connected in the fabric of the universe. Our spiritual connection will be covered at the end of the book. Have you conquered your feeling of aloneness? What does feeling lonely mean?

Jane does not like being alone, which is only compounding how she feels about being single. As she explores her loneliness, she realizes that, in part, she feels lonely because she seeks someone to comfort her when she is sad. It is as if she believes someone can fix the pain. She can learn to overcome her loneliness by discovering that only she can heal her sadness, and that no one else can fix it.

She also has come to realize that she feels alone because she has never felt as though she has received approval and acceptance, and that this lonely feeling is her longing for someone else to validate her. She can learn that only she can validate her own existence and that this is not a partner's job. She can realize that all too often we seek relationships to satisfy these neurotic needs. But this would not constitute an authentic relationship. An authentic relationship is sharing one's life with someone while not needing them to fill a neurotic need.

Mastering Emotions and Thoughts

He who knows others is wise; he who knows himself is enlightened.

-Loa-tzu

Once you have healed from your past and embraced the philosophies that have been illustrated, you achieve control over your thoughts and feelings, so you awaken to the reality that you have a choice as to how you feel. You have an opportunity right now to take charge of your life. Or you can remain a victim of your past and present circumstances. What are you going to choose? When something happens to you and you feel disappointed, hurt, upset, or whatever negative emotion, you choose these feelings, when you can just as easily choose not to feel them. This is a basic truth that is important to embrace to be able to move along the path of inner peace and personal growth. You have control over your thoughts and emotions, and by understanding them and wanting to change, you no longer have to be a victim of your past or current thoughts and feelings.

You now have the power to make changes. When you feel a negative emotion or thought arise, you can pause and ask yourself, "How can I see this differently or how can I feel differently." Remember, you have control over how you react to the situation. For example, if someone upsets you, you should ask yourself "Why am I upset?" Remembering that your current feelings are representations of past scars, you might conclude "I feel hurt because this person did something that triggered a feeling and a thought in me that I am not special, but I can control how I feel. This feeling of hurt is not productive. These feelings are not my current reality, but are based on my past, which I will not allow to color my present. I can let it go and not feel hurt." When you realize that you are responsible for your emotions, it changes how you deal with others, how you handle stressors, and how you feel.

If you find yourself still getting hurt by others or becoming distressed over external circumstances, this means that you need to spend just a little more time exploring the past and examining your feelings. The more you practice it, the easier it becomes. With time, these triggers will fade. You will start to create a sense of peace when you become more aware of your emotional life by understanding it and bringing it to consciousness. By doing this, you learn to gain control over your emotional state. This creates a foundation that stabilizes you when situations arise. You will learn to let go, which means making a conscious choice not to feel specific negative emotions. You acknowledge that they no longer serve a purpose.

When we are at peace, we are not avoiding our feelings, nor are they ruling us; rather, we are living in the middle ground. We become the wise mind that integrates the rational and the emotional. It is the serenity one can achieve when we become free from our emotions, thoughts, expectations, societal pressures, and external sources. Inner peace is what one feels after discovering life meaning, destiny, and purpose. When you have found the guiding principle in your life, and the feeling of empowerment, this is inner peace. Inner peace is the end-result of satisfying the basic human need of spirituality, which we will now explore.

Remember that change is difficult, so this change of paradigm is something that needs to be practiced. Often, we forget that our thoughts and feelings are hardwired in our brains. Our thoughts create synaptic pathways, and by thinking the same thoughts over and over again, we reinforce the physical connections.

Let us examine the route you take to work. When you first started your job, you had to be mindful of how to get to work. After working there for weeks, months, or years, you could probably get there in your sleep. Maybe one day you were extremely tired, yet you made it home without actually recalling how you got there. This happens because of the neural pathways that you created over time. Have you ever gone somewhere near your work on a day off and taken a wrong turn, actually winding up going to your office because you were on autopilot? In order to get to the other destination, you would have to think deeply about the path to overcome past programming.

Now, say you have a new job, with a different route. If you were then to return to your old place of work, after several months, it would not be automatic, and would take active thinking. This is how our brain works. It works this way with our thoughts and feelings as well.

We continually reinforce our thoughts and feelings, which is why they seem so difficult to change. We can look at our thoughts and feelings as habits, but we can retrain the brain with conscious and intentional living.

Reflection

One of the steps of discovering inner peace is committing to a life guided by philosophical principles, which assists you in living consciously and with intention. This is something that needs to be practiced regularly. How will you practice these techniques? What techniques can you use to serve as a reminder as to the philosophical principles you will incorporate into your life?

Some of the philosophical principles that can help us achieve inner peace include:

We can only control ourselves, not external factors.

We need to let go of expectations and desires, which means not being attached to the outcome of situations.

We can find inner peace by living in the present moment, not lamenting over the past or worrying about the future.

We are in control of our pain and nobody can hurt us unless we allow it.

Only you can validate your own existence.

You can find inner peace by being authentic and not playing a role.

Inner peace is found by living in a life-affirming way, not based on fear.

EMBRACING YOUR SPIRITUAL SIDE AND PRACTICING SPIRITUALITY

We are not human beings having a spiritual experience; we are spiritual beings having a human experience.

-Teilhard de Chardin

The final destination on the road to discovering inner peace is to embrace your spiritual side and practice spirituality. Through the process of discovering your spirituality, you can find the place of inner peace. As mentioned above, these spiritual messages have been around for thousands of years, yet we do not always hear or practice them for many reasons.

One reason is that we are too overwhelmed by our emotions and thoughts, which prevent us from fully understanding and applying the principles. Furthermore, we are addicted to the human drama, our thoughts and feelings and have difficulty detaching ourselves from them.

The first step is to heal from our past and gain mastery over our thoughts and emotions, before we can continue along the path of spiritual enlightenment This key principle is one I think many spiritual leaders lack in their teachings, meaning that they are not fully addressing the factors that prevent individuals from being in a place to embrace their messages. This is where I foresee psychology taking a critical part in the spiritual process.

Likewise, I believe that neglecting spiritual concerns during the psychological healing process is equally problematic. In order to assist individuals in achieving self-actualization, it is not just enough to decrease the symptoms of depression or anxiety. It is important to continue the process of individual growth and work to guide the individual to optimal well-being. The psychology process of healing from the past is the first step in the journey of discovering inner peace. Once you have started the process of healing and starting to apply life philosophies, you can continue your journey of inner peace by embracing and practicing spirituality.

What is Spirituality?

Spirituality is a domain of awareness.
                                        - Deepak Chopra.

The final step in discovering inner peace is to recognize that we are spiritual beings. It is important to first understand that being a spiritual being means committing to a life of spirituality.

Spirituality is an ambiguous term and may mean different things to different people, and it is important to discover how to live in a spiritual way. Spirituality can be seen as a way of life. It is the process of exploring who and what we are, and how we are all alike and connected together as humans. Spirituality is identifying the essence of who we are and living from our deepest nature, which includes being consciously aware of our thoughts and feelings and the impact we have on the world. Spirituality is living in harmony with the universe and understanding that we are all connected to each other because our spiritual essence is energy and we are all interconnected. This has profound implications.

We sometimes find it difficult to believe that we affect the universe in any way, but we have to always keep in mind that we are all energy and we need to understand that energy affects surrounding energy. We are connected to the universe. We have a responsibility to it; therefore, it is our duty to add to the universe something positive. Healing our emotional scars and being happy or at peace is actually part of our spiritual commitment to the universe. All too often, we feel that self-love or being happy or at peace is "selfish," but if we are part of a greater whole, we need to love ourselves just as much as we love others. Because we are impacting the world around us, being unhappy or living with fear, guilt or anger is in a sense adding negativity to our world. Therefore, it is our spiritual obligation to be happy and at peace, which we accomplish first by healing our wounds.

Sometimes we think that we are too insignificant to make any profound changes in the world. If we all just did our part, we could change the whole system quite dramatically. Being spiritual means connecting to the collective consciousness. It means understanding that we are creators and we own a creative force, which is powerful. However, we need to be conscious and mindful of our creations and to create something positive and out of love, not based on neurotic desires.

We can live spiritually by understanding that we are more than just the material—our physical self—but that we are energy as well. It is living in the middle ground, whereby we live a life that is in balance with both the material and the ethereal worlds. Spirituality means understanding how to live in harmony with our self and our true nature, which is living in alignment with our physical, emotional, and spiritual selves. We commit to a life that is balanced within ourselves, by making decisions that satisfy both the feeling and logical parts of us.

This recognition of our essence and letting go of the ego, which is our attachment to our physical selves, can be considered a spiritual awakening, or enlightenment. Believe it or not, everything that you have done so far—healing and changing—has already created this transformative process because we have healed those wounds that prevent us from living spiritually in the first place.

This spiritual awakening allows us to get in touch with the essence of who we are. We often mistake religion for spirituality, but there is a very clear distinction. Religion, for the most part, does not necessarily facilitate discovering one's spirit. Religion tends to set guidelines for behavior and leans toward separating people. Spirituality is about embracing the essence of who we are. This is the message behind all religions, but it is often lost in their doctrinal teachings. It is this connection to our spiritual side that helps us remain at peace, so it is essential.

Living Spiritually

Who looks outside, dreams; who looks inside, awakens.
                                                        –Carl Jung

Living spiritually is something that can be practiced every moment of our lives. The first step is exploring the ideas of spirituality and embracing our spirituality cognitively and emotionally. It is the understanding that inner peace is important not just because it is being taught to you, but because you intuitively know that you have been seeking it, and at times, have experienced it for yourself.

If there is any skepticism about this process, it is important to continue exploring it because it is your thoughts and feelings which are preventing you from finding peace. Spirituality is something that one needs to experience, not just read about. The good news is that there is no doing; it is more about just being. As we understand and experience it, we become more enlightened.

The first question is, are you ready to make some significant changes, because living a spiritual life may be something so different from what you have experienced before?

Putting the Ego In It's Place

Spiritual realization is to see clearly that what I perceive, experience, think or feel is ultimately not who I am, that I cannot find myself in all those things that continually pass away… what remains in the light of consciousness in which perceptions, experiences, thoughts and feelings come and go.

-Eckhardt Tolle

To fully achieve inner peace and start to live spiritually, it begins with the recognition that you are a spiritual being, and that being human means navigating both the material and the spiritual worlds. We often forget that the physical or earthly realm is only a part of who we are. This neglect of our spiritual side prevents us from achieving inner peace for many reasons.

One reason is that we identify too much with our ego, but it is our ego that creates our suffering and prevents us from finding peace. Our ego, until now, is who we think we are, which is only a small part of who we actually are. Everything we have done thus far was to heal the ego, because it is the wounded ego that gets in our way of finding inner peace. If we only identify with the ego, we creates a false sense of who we are because it is based on who we think we are, as created in our minds, which we have discovered is faulty and inaccurate.

Our ego or who we think we are, is based on past experiences. But who you are in this moment, is not based on past experiences, because these past experiences only exist in the mind, not reality. Who you are, is who you are in this moment, not a collection of thoughts based on past experiences. This is quite a profound shift in how we think about ourselves because most of us identify with who we think we are, which is not based on present reality. This leads us to be trap in a certain idea about ourselves, but at any moment, we can choose to just be who we are. This is part of the process of letting go of the ego.

The ego identifies itself based on external sources, such as possessions, job, status, etc., but these things are not you. The ego is always looking outward for happiness and answers and, as we discussed earlier, there are many problems in searching outside ourselves for happiness. Our ego is attached to that which is physical and material, and it is important to understand that there is so much more to who we are than just our physicality, just as there is more to the world than just the material.

The ego has a hard time living in the present because who we are, according to the ego, is always based on our past. Plus the ego judges the present reality. The ego also lives in the future, because it has expectations and desires—such as money, power, and fame—preventing us from being at peace within the moment. When we embrace our spirituality, we are able to see that we are more than our ego, and this allows us to fully let go of it. Once we let go of the ego, only then can we find enlightenment and spiritual awakening. The key is utilizing the ego to navigate our material world, but always knowing that it is the spirit, which is who you are, that is in the driver's seat. When we are not conscious of this, all too often, it is our ego who is doing the driving, which makes us unhappy. Living a spiritual life is putting the essence of who you are in the driver's seat, not the ego.

In order to embrace our spiritual side, part of the process of letting go of the ego is to separate ourselves from our thoughts, allowing us to discover our true essence. One of the reasons we identify with our ego is that we believe that who we are is who we think we are. However, we are not our thoughts, so we are not necessarily who we think we are. This may be a hard concept to grasp, but here is an experiment to illustrate this idea. Think about something, anything. Now think about something different. If you were your thoughts, would you really be able to, at one moment, think of something and then change your thought? You know that you have changed your minds about something. So, who is doing the changing? You are. You, then are not your thoughts, if in fact you can change them. You, are something greater than your thoughts. You, the essence of who you are, is what we can define as consciousness. This idea of the "I" is a very interesting one. Scientists have discovered that when we have a thought or feeling, certain parts of the brain are active. For years, scientists have tried to find the part of the brain in which the "I" exists. They have not yet found it, which is part of the spiritual mystery.

Earlier, we discussed how to challenge our thoughts, so we know that when a thought arises, we can challenge and change it. We can also change our feelings. If we can do that, it proves that we are not our thoughts or feelings. There is something else: an essence of who we are, our spirit or consciousness, which can control our thoughts and our feelings. You can control the thinker, who, by the way, is the one who is making you miserable. Once you become conscious of this, you can start to achieve peacefulness, because it is our thoughts and consequent feelings that prevent us from finding inner peace. It is important that we are in control of our thoughts, not vice versa, as our thoughts keep us from achieving peace in our lives. Our thoughts and feelings are conditioned by the past, not by present reality, which is why they can sometimes distress us.

It is also the ego that feels superior to the natural flow of things and therefore feels separate from others and the universe, which creates a feeling of being incomplete and lonely. Once we understand that we are all connected, we can start to perceive others, as well as our place within the universe, in a different light. If we are a part of the whole, there is no distress. Distress comes in when we feel isolated and separate from the rest of the world. Distress is when we believe in an "I" against the world idea. When we embrace the idea that I am part of the whole, there is trust and hence no distress. There is trust that everything will work out and I will be provided for. When we trust, we can learn that when obstacles come our way, there is a spiritual reason for it. Everything that enters into your world can now be seen as a lesson to be learned, not something that you need to be upset over. So, when adversity strikes, instead of feeling distressed, when we trust, we can look at these obstacles and ask, "What do I need to learn about myself right now?" and "Why am I manifesting this in my universe?"

Once we let go of the ego, we can become compassionate with others and understand that we are connected to one another, leading us to love each other, not hate or judge, because we understand that hatred and judgment is negative energy that hurts you just as much as it hurts others. When we hate or are angry, this just imparts negativity within our universe. It is sometimes difficult to not judge and be angry when we see injustice and when others are suffering. However, peace can be attained when we understand that everything happens for a reason, even the terrible things and judging or hating those who are "bad," is still imparting negativity to our world. When we let go of the ego, we need to also let go of judgment, which if you really think about it, is hurting you more than solving any problems.

When we are able to put aside the ego, we come from a place of wisdom, and are able to see a bigger picture. We are able to see that we are part of a bigger whole and can make decisions that do not merely satisfy the needs of the ego. When we can let go of our ego, we can put things in perspective. We can see how insignificant some of the drama that we encounter truly is in the grand scheme of things. Letting go of the ego allows us to enjoy the simple things and be grateful for what we have, not what we do not have.

Furthermore, when you feel superior or separate from the universe, you will judge the present and not accept it. Inner peace, which comes when you can accept your present reality without judgment, will elude you. When we let go of the ego, we no longer try to control things outside of ourselves. We can also cast off our beliefs of how things should be and accept life as it is, finding peace within. So instead of striving for perfection in life, which is dictated by our egos, we can just live life. There is a place of peacefulness that can be achieved when you start to accept your present circumstance, even when the present circumstance is terrible. Stress is created when we struggle in accepting what is. This does not mean, however, that you cannot strive to change your situation. It means that you can try to make changes without feeling stress.

This concept of letting go of our ego and material things is essentially preparing us for the ultimate letting go—death. Once we fully embrace our spiritual side, we can no longer fear death, because our spirit, essence of who we are, or energy will always be there, even though our physical aspect may not. There is a peacefulness to be found when you understand this because much of the anxiety that we have centers on the fear of death. But if we embrace the essence of who we are, death is just the end of the material part of who we are. If we are not attached to the materiality of who we are, we can find peace when we understand that we are in a sense immortal. As we know, energy cannot be destroyed nor created, only transformed. Therefore, the essence of who you are has and always will be. Death is only the death of the physical part of who we are, not the spiritual part.

Since our material world is largely created by our ego, it is important to continually practice connection and detachment from the ego. Relaxation practices such as meditation can be helpful, because it helps you practice remaining centered, which is good practice to prepare you for a time of adversity. Centering brings strength to reach within instead of getting caught up in what is happening outside. Training yourself to slow down is quite helpful in taking control over yourself and your life. When you learn to slow down, you take control of yourself, instead of letting external factors, such as modern living, dictating how you should lead your life.

If you truly seek to be free and with true freedom you can find peace, you need to be free from our thoughts, feelings and societal constraints. All of these are housed in our egos.

It is important to understand that we all have an ego, which is not a bad thing. We are human and we need the ego to navigate our world and, in fact, we need the ego to heal our scars and to grow. But it is important to not allow the ego to control our lives. We need to understand that the ego, if not put in perspective, will prevent us from finding peace. Our ego is not the all of who we are, and it is important to continually practice letting the ego go. So when negative feelings arise, think to yourself, "Is this my ego that is controlling me?" It usually is.

Living In Harmony with the Universe and Being the Creator of Your Life

We must be willing to let go of the life we have planned, so as to accept the life that is waiting for us.

- *Joseph Cambell*

Living as a spiritual being is always being mindful that you are apart of the universe and it is important to live every moment understanding this premise. Once the ego is no longer controlling your life, you can now take a totally new approach to living. You can start to live consciously and, with this consciousness, you become the creator of your life. When you are the creator, you are no longer the victim of circumstances. This is true and authentic empowerment, whereby you seek empowerment in your own life, not seeking power over others or other things.

To understand that we are creators takes a change in paradigm. We are raised believing that the world is bigger and more powerful than we are. We also believe that we are in the world. Therefore, to find out who I am, I think that I need to explore the external world. This idea prevents us from looking within for the answers, but the universe within us is where the answers truly are. Science has shown us very interesting evidence that suggests just how powerful we are. All matter, in terms of quantum physics, exists in a wave of possibilities. It is only when the observer, of the "I," fixates on a point that it materializes. Therefore, without the observer, even material objects would not exist as we know it. It is only when we perceive something that it actually begins to exist in reality. You know that if you close your eyes, what exists in your minds is really no different than what you actually see. This has profound implications how powerful we are. This shift in perspective can help you understand just how powerful you truly are and that it just may be that we are put here to be our own creators.

As we live our lives, we should always seek to live in harmony with the universe because we are one with the universe. When we are able to live harmoniously with the universe, there is no stress, because we are connected to the universal flow of things. Being in the flow is allowing things to come to us and approaching life gently, with the least resistance.

We should strive to create our life through intention and be flexible in that we embrace what is given to us and contribute positive things to our environment. It is also trusting that the universe will provide for you what you need as long as you are living in harmony with it. It is important not to resist the natural rhythms of things and focus on what you need to do and wait for what will be created, because it is a much more peaceful place when you go with the flow of the universe. It is the idea of setting aside our ego, which says, "I know what is best," because sometimes the universe may just have other plans and fighting it only creates distress.

There is power in the universal flow of things of which we need to be conscious. It is not that we are powerless, because as mentioned before, we are the creators, but it is in our best interest to sometimes surrender and go with the flow as we are interconnected. It is not that we should not have goals, but to trust that the universe will provide a path for us, if we are patient. Even in the midst of adversity, it is important to be centered and patient. Oftentimes, we learn our most valuable lessons in the face of adversity and instead of fighting it, you can learn to be still and wait for the lesson that is to be learned. This idea may be very foreign to you because we usually operate in a way that we believe that we are removed from the universe. We have to do, go get things and make things happen instead of allowing the process to happen. So, how does this translate into your life? When you find yourself in an adverse situation, it is being in that place and doing what you need to do and not worrying how it will be executed because the universe will guide your way.

If you are a part of a bigger picture, with that comes trust, because there is no one or nothing else having power over you. It is all harmonious. There is peace when you let go and trust that the universe will unfold the path for you, which is a different approach to life, especially in terms of goals. There is no more idea of goal setting, but instead the notion of living in synergy with the universe. Instead of being goal oriented, just do what you need to do—be and experience life. We should always strive to keep our focus on what we have to do in the moment, adding something positive to the universe and the end result will manifest itself. We do not have to worry about the end result, as we tend to worry too much about the future. This worry is an indication that we do not trust that our universe will provide us for what we truly need, which is sometimes different from what we want.

This wanting is attachment to the ego. We need to focus on living in harmony with our world, because we are part of a bigger picture, not separate from it. We should strive to create our life through intention and be flexible in that we embrace what is given to us and contribute positive things to our environment. It is also important not to resist the natural rhythms of things and focus on what you need to do and wait for what will be created, because it is a much more peaceful place when you go with the flow of the universe.

Because you are the creator and you are part of a bigger picture, it is important that you are mindful of your creation, which means always acting for the greater good and imparting only positive things. There is no room for negative feelings, such as hate and judgment, because this is negative energy which ultimately impacts us.

You are the creator, which means you always have a choice in everything you do. There is nothing you "have" to do, as often we are stressed about those tasks that may not be congruent with our true nature. You can create the life you want: an authentic life, not a life based on satisfying neurotic needs. You must ask yourself if you truly believe that you can have the life that you want and that everything you do you chose to do. If there are doubts, it is important to address them.

Spirituality is experiencing life, observing and learning with wisdom. Wisdom is not believing that you know everything, but being humble and understanding that you are aware that you don't have all of the answers. However, part of this spiritual journey is listening to that inner voice to assist in charting your course and navigating the universe. It is important to approach life with humility, understanding that this is a journey of discovery and being in the mystery.

One way that we can practice spirituality is to be more present in nature. Being in nature is truly a humbling experience. You can see the synergy of how the world works together. This is important because it is our ego that is destroying nature or feeling the need to enhance it in some way. Indeed, we are seeing the devastating effects of not preserving and respecting nature. Being a part of nature also means connecting with your fellow man. We are all connected and need to open our hearts to all, not just those that think and act like us.

On your journey, it is important to strive for balance each day; living in alignment with our physical, emotional and spiritual selves. We can think of ill health or illnesses as signals that we are not in harmony with ourselves. Part of this spiritual awareness is finding the meaning in everything, including suffering. It is embracing the idea that growth happens in the face of adversity, and part of this spiritual journey is embracing our humanity. When there is adversity, this may be an indication that you are resisting the natural flow of life or not learning a lesson that the universe wants you to learn. It means being okay with being human.

So when faced with adversity, it is important to sit with the pain, fear, or whatever the emotion is, and work through it. All too often we try to escape our pain. But you can find strength and deal with it, having hope or faith and knowing that everything will be okay in spite of it. This hope or faith is synonymous with optimism. It means knowing that all things happen for a reason, and seeing the message behind the unpleasant things we are going through. This awareness is grounding, and helps one remain at peace.

On this journey, there will be times when you will not feel not at peace, ask yourself if you are identifying with the ego or neglecting your spiritual side? When negative feelings arise, you need to ask yourself, what is this about me that I still need to learn? Even if someone wrongs you, you need to explore why it hurts you. Remember, we are hurt when others wrong us because we believe that they shouldn't. Again, this is judgment, any judgment is negative energy. Actually now is the simple part of our journey if we realize that all distress is in regards to the ego.

Remember, peacefulness is something that needs to be practiced by living consciously, because it is easy to get involved with external things. The more you practice, the easier it will become. As you continue on your journey, at some point you may encounter a time when it is difficult to remain at peace. Now that you know that you have the power and the tools to create inner peace, you can continue on this journey, and that this too shall pass. Remember, inner peace is not the destination, but the journey to discover it. Once you experience inner peace, then you will understand just how profound it is.

Reflection

Our last step of discovering inner peace is to embrace our spiritual side and practice spirituality. We can embrace our spiritual side by letting go of the ego and absorbing the essence of who we are. What does spirituality mean for you? When does your ego prevent you from finding inner peace? How will you practice spirituality on a daily basis?

SUMMARY

There is one thing which, if practiced and developed, conduces to letting go, giving up, stilling, calming, higher knowledge, awakening and to Nirvana. And what is that one thing? It is the recollection of peace.

– The Buddha

You most likely picked up this book because you were seeking answers to questions that have been asked for centuries. You have started your own unique journey of discovering inner peace through self-awareness, healing and living more consciously. My wish for you is to take that scary first step to explore those things that you fear; to be able to look into the darkness and to confront those inner demons because on the other side, lies the treasure. Take this book on your journey with you as a reminder that we are all on a similar journey. However, we all need to walk that path alone, but to never forget that we are never truly alone if we all come from one source.

Although each of our journeys are unique, this book hopefully provides you with a framework in which you can reference as you move along your path. The first part of the journey is to heal from the past. This requires us to examine and understand the past and how it impacts us presently. We also need to process the feelings that create our suffering and let them go, which allows us to gain mastery over our thoughts and feelings in the present. This journey consists of a number of steps, including self-reflection, validation of your emotions, feeling your feelings, and challenging your beliefs and perceptions. Once you have healed from the past, you can start to live from a place of philosophical ideals and spirituality. You can begin to live a more conscious life, not being ruled by your ego and understanding the essence of who you truly are. As you continue your journey, I wish you peace and happiness.

EPILOGUE

There is a shift happening right now: a shift in consciousness, as if we are awakening to the state of the world we have created. We are examining our selves and the consequences of our actions. We are questioning the human condition as expressed through misery, hate, war, and human suffering. Many are making a choice to live more consciously through personal growth.

We have seen an intellectual evolution with the exploration of our world through scientific discovery. In the early part of the century, we also started to explore emotions and psychology, which led to an evolution in our understanding of our emotional selves. Now it appears as though we are encountering a spiritual evolution. Although throughout history there have been great philosophers and thinkers that addressed these concerns, many did not grasp its full importance.

Now, we are blending science with spirituality and starting to see the whole picture. We have spent thousands of years studying these elements separately, but now is a time of integration—integrating the logical, emotional, and spiritual parts of our being. Many new thinkers are integrating different theories, some old and some new, to get a better understanding of our world and our selves. It is as if the pieces of the puzzle have always been there, and now we are in a time where we can integrate these thoughts to see the full picture. There is a need to combine psychology, philosophy, and spirituality to heal the human condition.

Many believe that it is our duty to change the world because there is worldwide suffering that mankind has created. We are looking for world peace, but in order to have peace in the world the journey must start by finding peace within one's self. As Gandhi once said, "Be the change you want to see in the world." Therefore, the first step to world peace is inner peace.